NATIONAL GEOGRAPHIC

SPECTACLE

RARE AND ASTONISHING PHOTOGRAPHS

FOREWORD BY MARK THIESSEN

NATIONAL GEOGRAPHIC
WASHINGTON, D.C.

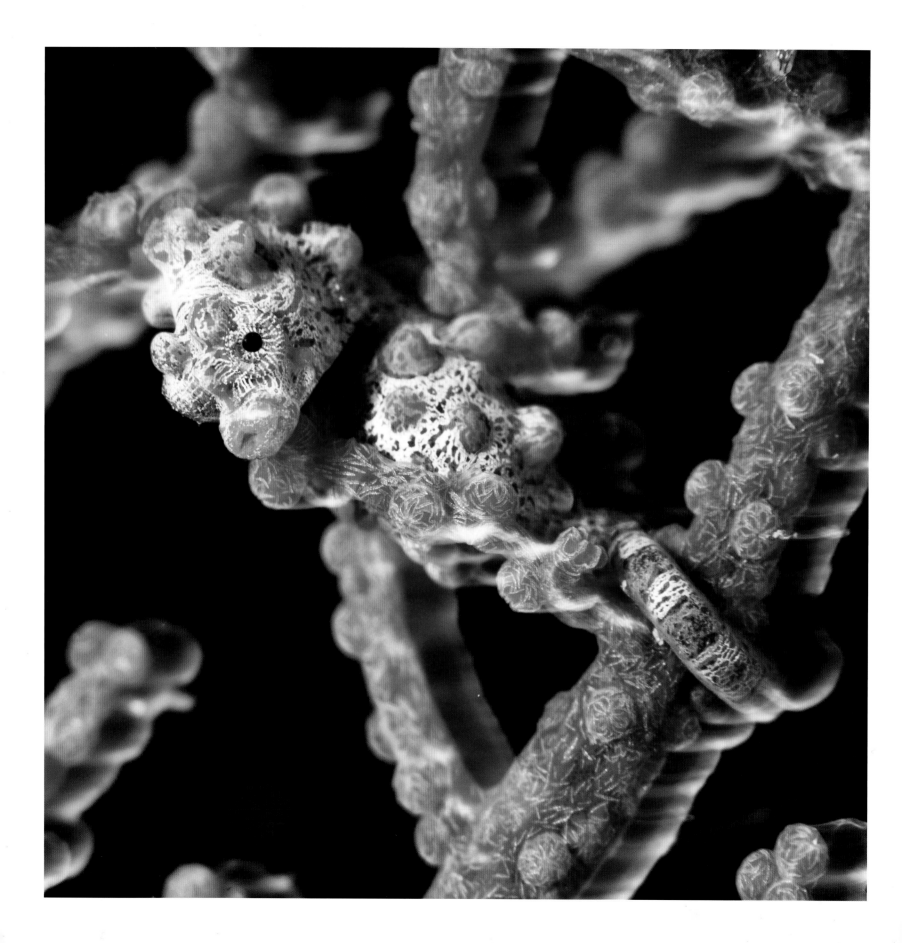

PAGE 1: **YASUNI NATIONAL PARK, ECUADOR** | *Tim Laman*
PAGES 2-3: **FUJIAN PROVINCE, CHINA** | *Danny Wong*
LEFT: **MABUL ISLAND, SABAH, MALAYSIA** | *Mauricio Handler*
PAGES 6-7: **ZHANGJIAJIE NATIONAL FOREST PARK, CHINA** | *Michael Yamashita*

PAGES 8-9: **KUALA LUMPUR, MALAYSIA** | *Manan Vatsyayana*
PAGES 10-11: **AMBER MOUNTAIN NATIONAL PARK, MADAGASCAR** | *Christian Ziegler*
PAGES 12-13: **UBON RATCHATHANI, THAILAND** | *Piyaphon Phemtaweepon*
PAGES 14-15: **NEW YORK, NEW YORK** | *Media Drum World*

FOREWORD

Suddenly things didn't feel right. The sky grew dark as the thick black smoke billowed across the sun, turning the woods an eerie orange. As we walked along the road, the forest floor began to snap, crackle, and pop as dry brush burst into flames. Next the trees nearby began torching, throwing massive amounts of heat, smoke, and embers over our heads. The roar grew louder, causing us to pick up the pace.

The wind had shifted. The firefighters' plan to stop the flames by burning out the vegetation between the road and the blazing front was not working; the unexpected wind change meant the inferno was coming right at us instead of burning up the mountainside as planned. Embers landed across the road and sparked spot fires to the other side of us. The division supervisor's radio crackled with reports that the flames had jumped the road in many places. It was time for us to bug out.

I was in my fourth week following wildland fire crews in the American West for an article in *National Geographic* magazine: in other words, trying to get into the middle of the fire fight. This was the moment I was waiting for.

As I hopped in the division supervisor's truck, all I could see was a wall of dark smoke ahead of us and fire on each side. I knew something was about to happen but didn't know exactly what. I braced my camera against my face and began to shoot pictures from the passenger seat. As we penetrated the wall of smoke, it opened to an otherworldly scene of flames all around our truck. I shot pictures like crazy. In that instant, I captured a surreal

WASHINGTON, D.C. I A high-speed strobe freezes the moment when a water balloon pops, leaving the water in the shape of the balloon. *(Mark Thiessen)*

moment that will live forever, and one I will never forget: the view from inside our vehicle surrounded by fire (see pages 374–375).

Every photographer dreams of capturing the instant when the light, composition, and action line up to create a spectacular photograph. These are the rare gems that cause you to question yourself. "Did I just take that picture? I'm not capable of taking that picture. It's just too good." These are the images guided by magic.

The book you hold in your hands is filled with spectacular moments just like this one, frozen in time for you to appreciate and enjoy. Curated with care by our National Geographic photo editors, it continues our tradition of presenting you, our readers, with the best photography in the world. These images awe and inspire, capturing our miraculous planet in all its glory. They include moments of celebration, from the brilliant colors of the Holi festival in India to fireworks exploding off the coast of Rio de Janeiro. They also reveal awe-inspiring life-forms, from the world's smallest reptile to a sea star feeding frenzy. You'll also experience moments of utter chaos, from volcanic lightning to a swirling, transparent vortex sweeping through Kansas fields. And if nothing else, you'll be surprised at the sight of a wave shot from the inside to a fish poking out from its soda-can home: a reminder of our human impact on the world.

Needless to say, the photography in these pages wasn't easy to achieve. Each shot took planning, commitment, dogged determination, sometimes dumb luck . . . and a little bit of magic. We hope you will enjoy experiencing them as much as we enjoyed creating them.

—**Mark Thiessen**

CLE ELUM, WASHINGTON | The Black Mesa Hotshots from Arizona work on the Jolly Mountain blaze, fighting fire with fire in a forest where water is scarce. *(Mark Thiessen)*

CHAOS

FORCES BEYOND US

Some photographs plunge into chaos. Chaos—from the ancient Greek for the nether abyss, the earliest of days, shape without form or meaning: It may be where it all started, but chaos looms in the corners and hovers in the moments of our lives every day.

Step out of the human comfort zone and into the world where nature rules: where thick roots, centuries old, clasp the doors and columns of deserted temples; where thousands of beings, filmy nothings and muscle-bound monsters, thrive in a watery world where, unprotected, we would perish; where waves crash, icebergs calve, and volcanoes spew fire and ash. There is no way we humans can hold back these forces. All we can do is watch with amazement, hold our breath, and go with the flow.

Or we might befriend the spirit. In medieval England a Lord of Misrule frolicked through the holidays, reminding celebrants things were not always as they seemed. Best, perhaps, to make friends with chaos: Admit to the law of entropy, where everything tends toward disorder; find pleasure and delight in the colors and shapes and overwhelming messiness of stuff.

OPPOSITE: **ABACO ISLAND, BAHAMAS** I Blacktip reef sharks enmesh with jacks and snappers in a well-attended feeding event off Walker's Cay in the Caribbean. *(Brian Skerry)*

PREVIOUS PAGES: **ICELAND** I Electric lightning bolts splinter across the evening sky as ash billows from the erupting Eyjafjallajökull volcano. *(Sigurdur H. Stefnisson)*

RIGHT: **TAIJIANG, GUIZHOU PROVINCE, CHINA** | Revelers shower marchers in a parade celebrating the Fire Dragon Lunar New Year Festival. *(Christian Kober)*

PAGE 26: **GREELEY COUNTY, KANSAS** | A tornado's translucent vortex swirls from monster storm clouds, bridging an indigo sky to touch down in an unspoiled wheat field. *(Jim Reed)*

PAGE 27: **HVERARÖND, ICELAND** | The mighty gush of steam vents fans into the sky and blends with the ethereal emeralds of the northern lights seen from Námafjall. *(Orsolya Haarberg)*

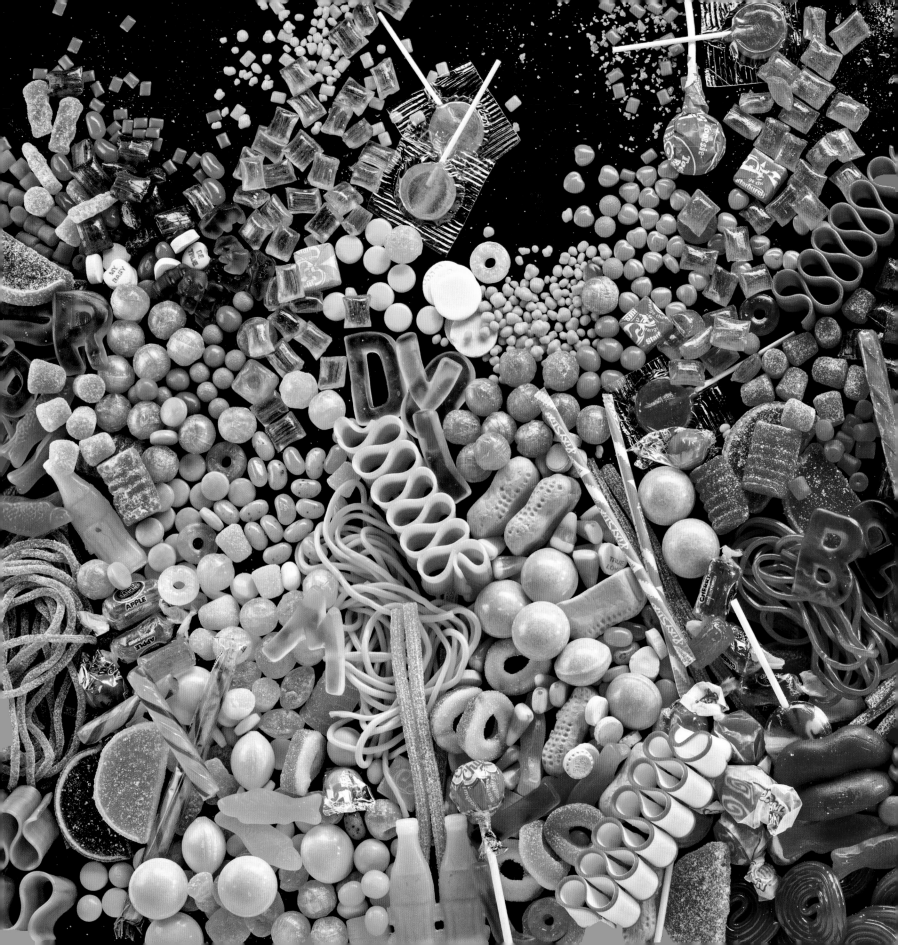

LEFT: **UTTAR PRADESH, INDIA |** A hot pink haze envelops revelers already caked in the chromatic powders tossed about at Holi festival, an annual Hindu religious tradition that ushers in springtime. *(Philippe Michel)*

PREVIOUS PAGES: **BROOKLYN NAVY YARD, BROOKLYN, NEW YORK |** Purple lollipops, red chews, green gummies: A rainbow of candy flaunts sugar's innumerable—and irresistible—shapes. *(Robert Clark)*

31

ARCHITECTURE CAN'T FULLY REPRESENT
THE CHAOS AND TURMOIL THAT ARE
PART OF THE HUMAN PERSONALITY,
BUT YOU NEED TO PUT SOME OF THAT
TURMOIL INTO THE ARCHITECTURE,
OR IT ISN'T REAL.

FRANK STELLA

SIEM REAP, CAMBODIA I Silk-cotton and strangler fig tree roots grip the ancient stones of Ta Prohm, joining moss and creeping plants in the jungle's siege on the Buddhist temple of Angkor Wat. *(Robert Clark)*

LEFT: **REPUBLIC OF PALAU, CAROLINE ISLANDS** | A diver disappears amid a throng of jellyfish seeking sunlight in one of the Pacific archipelago's many marine lakes. *(David Doubilet)*

FOLLOWING PAGES: **INTERNATIONAL SPACE STATION** | An astronaut's view turns London's sprawl into a fractal beauty of twinkling lights, tangles of roads, and undeveloped pockets of darkness, with the serpentine Thames River carving the center. *(Tim Peake)*

HEFEI, CHINA | Rows of student chefs supervise the flames that blossom from their woks while they practice preparing vegetables at blistering temperatures. *(Fritz Hoffmann)*

DORSET, ENGLAND | Seagulls help themselves to an order of English chips (french fries), enjoying their post on a wall in West Bay on a clear afternoon. (Martin Parr)

NOVOSIBIRSK, RUSSIA I A brown rat heaves itself upright in a flash of anger that attests its hostility toward humans, a behavior for which it's been bred. *(Vincent J. Musi)*

ZAMBEZI RIVER, ZIMBABWE | A crew of rafters tumbles into white water after fierce Class V rapids below Victoria Falls best its boat. *(Chris Johns)*

43

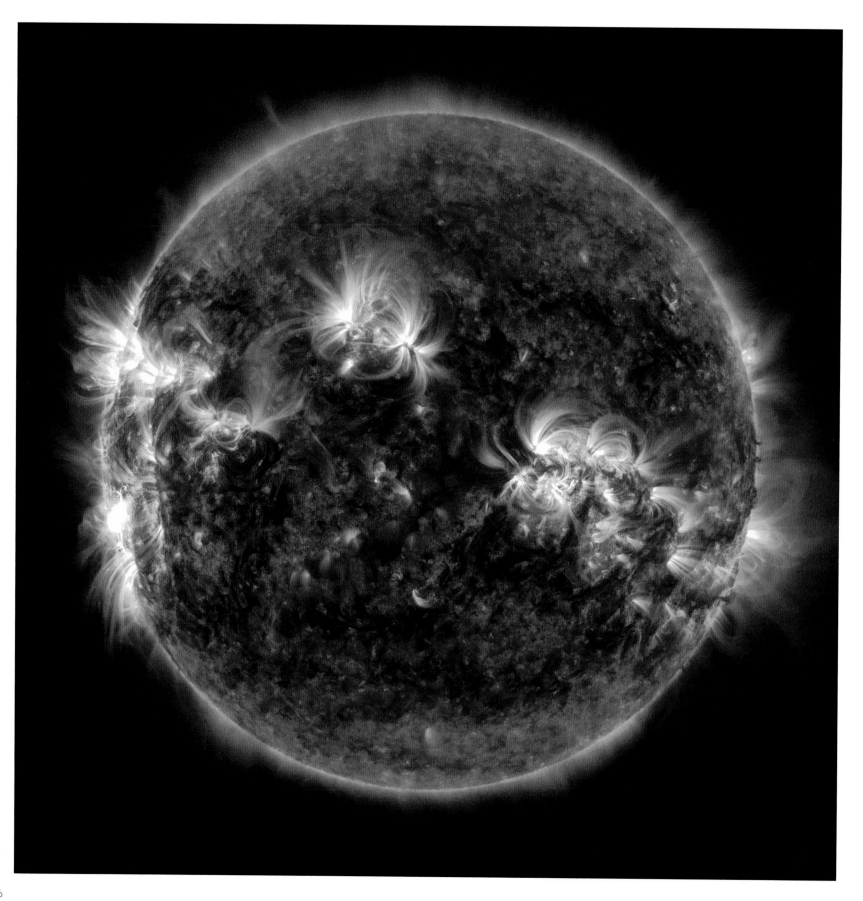

IN PLAIN WORDS, CHAOS WAS THE LAW OF NATURE; ORDER WAS THE DREAM OF MAN.

HENRY ADAMS

OPPOSITE: **SPACE** | Sparkles on a golden orb represent X-class solar flares, intense winds the sun emitted and NASA's Solar Dynamics Observatory captured in 171 angstrom light. *(NASA/SDO)*

PREVIOUS PAGES: **VERZY, FRANCE** | The curved limbs of Faux de Verzy, or dwarf beech trees, create a twisting, snow-dusted web as they fuse with neighboring branches in a protected area. *(Christophe Boisvieux)*

**AHMADABAD, INDIA | ** Steadied by a rope, a worker is swallowed in
a cloud of white as he stamps down cotton fibers separated from their
seeds and blown clean by a fan at a local ginning factory. *(Cary Wolinsky)*

CORNWALL, ENGLAND | Waves spray over rock in powder white jets when a winter storm churns the ocean around the Penwith peninsula. *(David Clapp)*

RIGHT: **ORGANYÀ, SPAIN** | Pilot and wing flip-flop as a paraglider performs a stunt called infinity tumbling over the Pyrenees in Catalonia. *(Brooke Whatnall)*

FOLLOWING PAGES: **PHOENIX, ARIZONA** | A 5,000-foot wall of dust, or a haboob, approaches Phoenix on a July evening, dividing the city between windswept fury and anticipatory stillness. *(Mike Olbinski)*

54

SEOUL, SOUTH KOREA I Whirling glow sticks make neon abstractions around performers at Everland theme park during its "Cyber Jwibulnoli," an event that precedes the first full moon of the Lunar New Year. *(Chung Sung-Jun)*

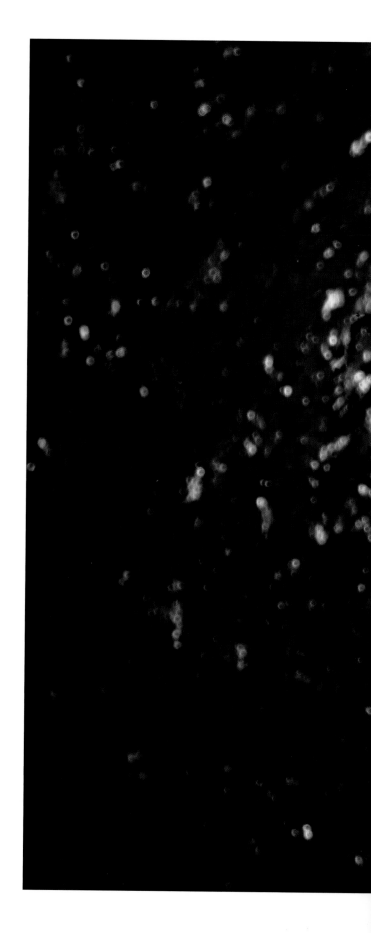

RIGHT: **MASAI MARA NATIONAL RESERVE, KENYA** I
An African buffalo's features are veiled after a cooling roll
around a mudhole. *(Chris Schmid)*

PAGE 58: **KILAUEA, HAWAII** I Hurrying across hours-old lava,
a researcher from the Hawaiian Volcano Observatory quickly
collects samples at Mauna Ulu during its multiphase eruption.
(Robert Madden)

PAGE 59: **PAMPLONA, SPAIN** I Daredevils donning traditional
white garb and red scarves stake their lives to run with the bulls,
corralling the riled cattle toward the ring where they will fight as
part of the San Fermín Festival. *(Emanuele Ciccomartino)*

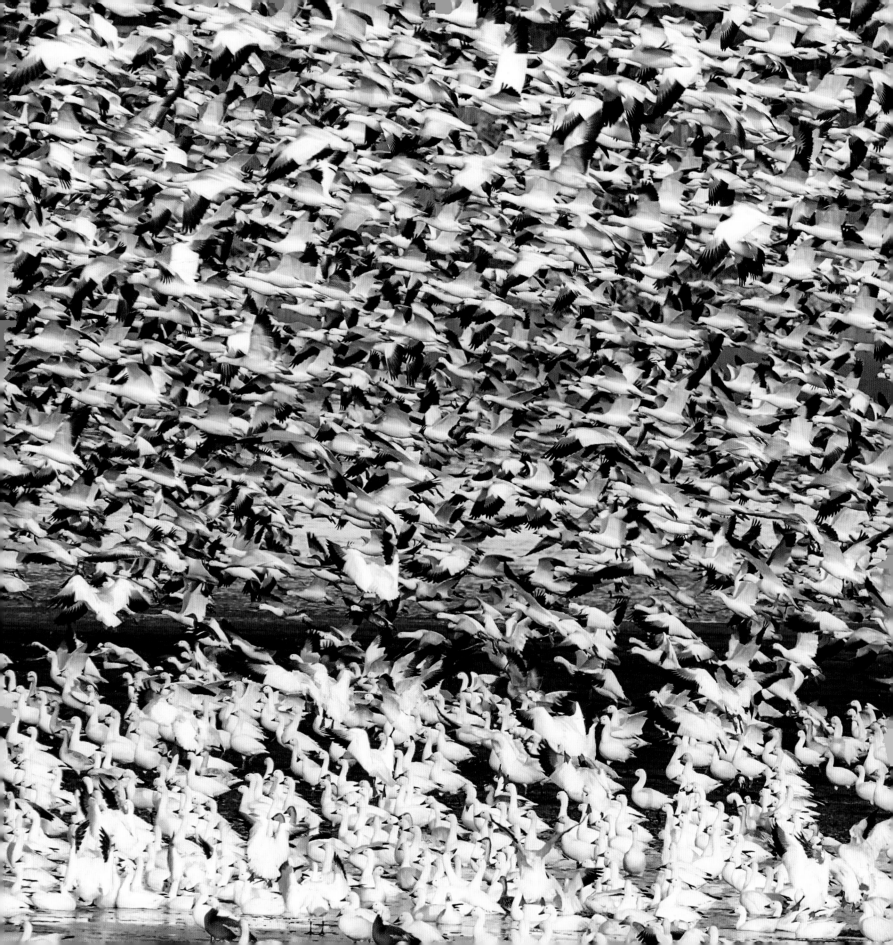

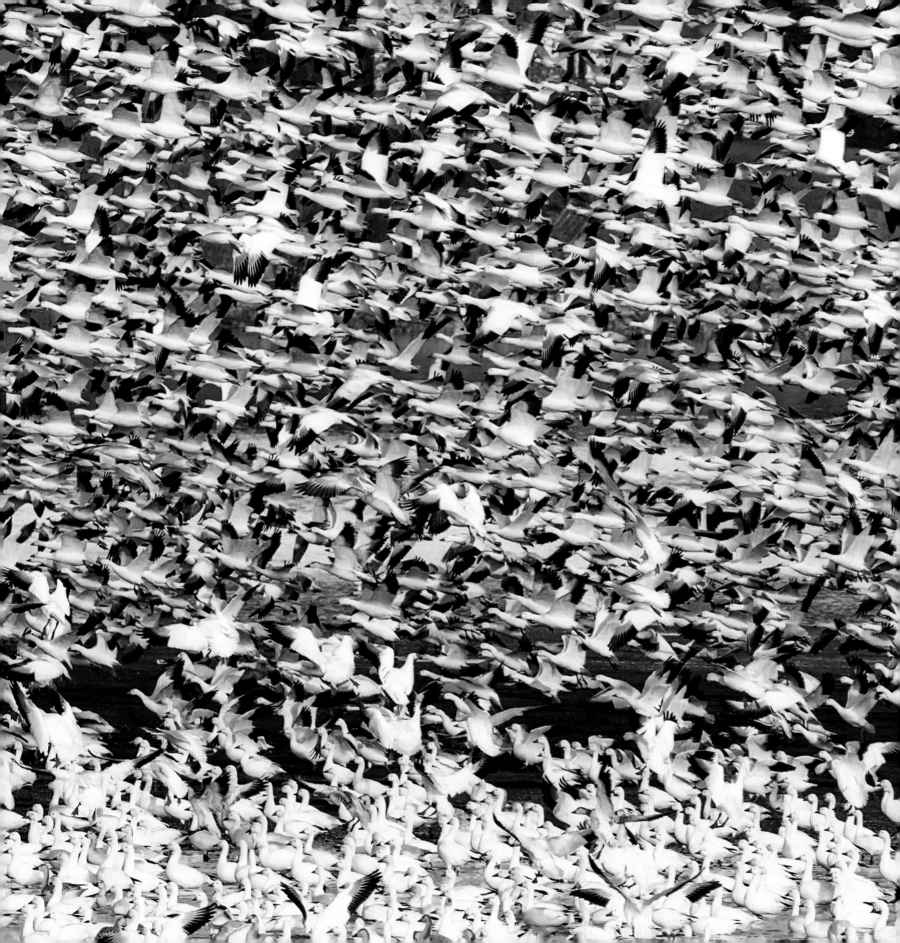

LEFT: **NEPTUNE ISLANDS, AUSTRALIA** | Rows of spiked teeth and a gaping pink jaw: The bite of a great white shark upholds its fearsome reputation on an underwater cage's metal corner. *(Julian Cohen)*

PREVIOUS PAGES: **QUEBEC, CANADA** | Greater snow geese alight on the St. Francis River, dropping from the teeming flock in a blur of blue and white for a rest from their long migration. *(David Doubilet)*

EVERY CHAOS HAS AN ORDER HIDDEN
IN IT. WHAT WE SEE AS A CHAOS,
IS ACTUALLY DRIVEN BY
A VERY DISCIPLINED AND
DEDICATED ORDER OF THINGS.

SAPAN SAXENA

OBWALDEN, SWITZERLAND | Flecks of red on a smooth white canvas, skiers glide down an immaculate slope
in an inverted pyramid formation that reflects the Alpine peaks overhead. *(Robert Bösch)*

LEFT: **EAST JAVA, INDONESIA** | Following an alert of seismic activity, Gunung Bromo spews smoke and ash at sunrise and hangs a miasma of orange and gray over Bromo-Tengger-Semeru National Park. *(Reynold Riksa Dewantara)*

FOLLOWING PAGES: **LAGOS, NIGERIA** | Motor traffic doesn't stall the flow of pedestrians who have buying and selling to do at a street market in the booming Surulere District. *(Yann Arthus-Bertrand)*

RIGHT: **BLACK ROCK CITY, NEVADA** I A 20-foot-tall boar cast in steel and christened "Lord Snort" provides a playground for "Burners" during the Burning Man festival's annual bacchanalia. (*Aaron Huey*)

PAGE 72: **ALBERTA, CANADA** I Peeling, water-stained wallpaper in an abandoned prairie home epitomizes the disrepair of what remains in Nemiskam, a ghost town off of Highway 61. (*Pete Ryan*)

PAGE 73: **SPACE SATELLITE** I Prevailing winds diverted by land spiral into a chain of eddies known as von Kármán vortices amid the tufts of clouds over Guadalupe Island. (*NASA*)

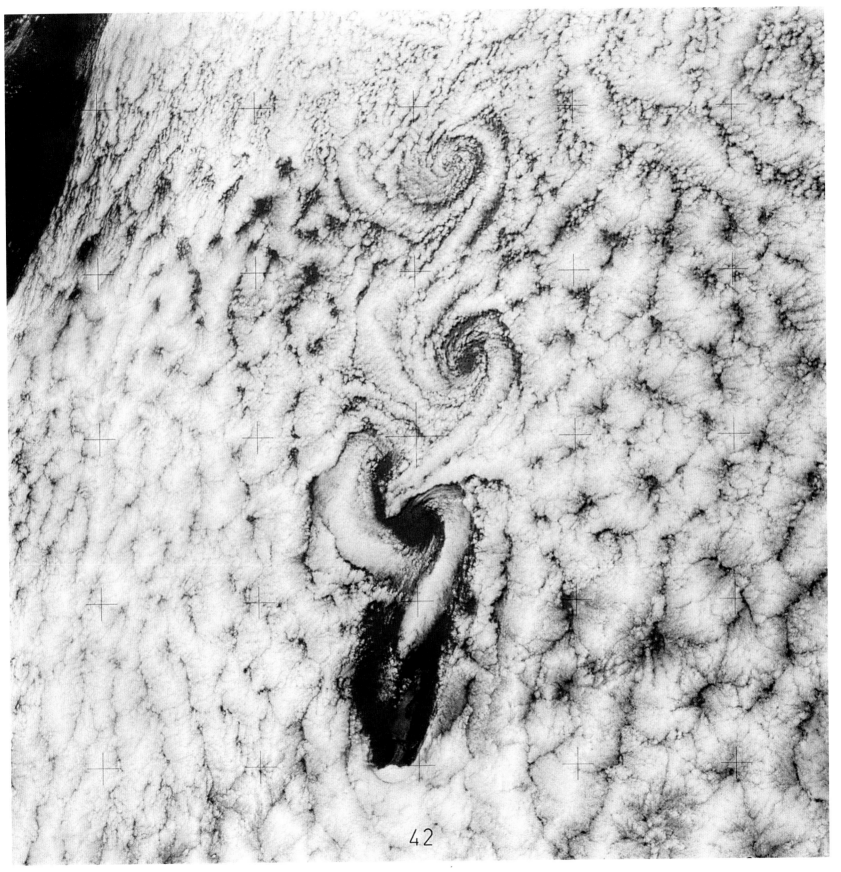

42

LEFT: **SINDH, PAKISTAN** | Silk webs cocoon treetops after drenching monsoon rains submerged the countryside, sending millions of spiders and other insects up to dry branches. *(Russell Watkins)*

FOLLOWING PAGES: **MUNICH, GERMANY** | A glittering mélange of hand-painted Christmas ornaments and baubles hides its vendor at a holiday market. *(Veronika K Ko)*

BEIJING, CHINA | A bike-share company employee hoists a damaged bicycle onto the heap awaiting repair at a local depot, evidence of the growing popularity of the urban transport system. *(Kevin Frayer)*

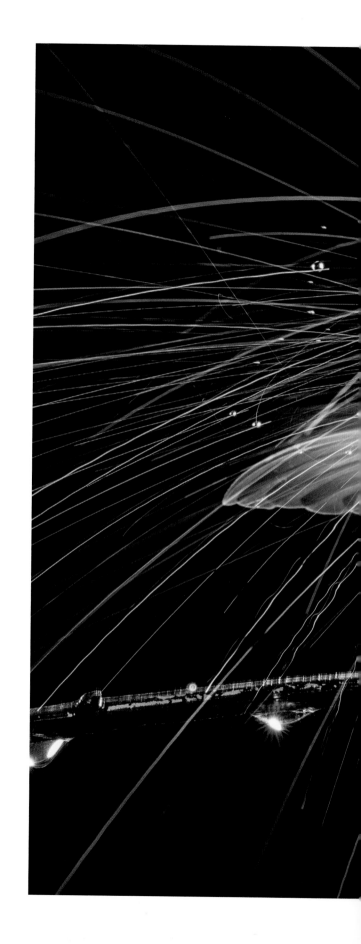

BERKELEY, CALIFORNIA I Water droplets streak like comet tails
across the sky as an Anna's hummingbird shakes off simulated rain,
oscillating its head and body in rapid-fire motion. *(Anand Varma)*

JUNEAU, ALASKA l A lone walker braces against powerful
afternoon gusts and snowdrift as the infamous Taku winds
bear down on Savikko Park. *(Mark Kelley)*

ALICANTE, SPAIN | A blizzard of flour and eggs sweeps the small town of Ibi during the Els Enfarinats festival. Residents dress in military attire and do battle with raw ingredients, firecrackers, and fire extinguishers. *(Antonio Gibotta)*

LEFT: **SAN DIEGO, CALIFORNIA | ** At the San Diego Padres home opener against the San Francisco Giants, the stadium erupts in festivity as the national anthem is sung. *(Stephen Dunn)*

PREVIOUS PAGES: **KENYA | ** A packed herd of Grant's zebras makes an undulating pattern of stripes as it nears the treacherous Mara River, which it must cross to continue its migration. *(Art Wolfe)*

CHAOS IS NOT THE LACK OF ORDER,
IT IS MERELY THE ABSENCE OF ORDER,
THAT THE OBSERVER IS USED TO.

MAMUR MUSTAPHA

DHAKA, BANGLADESH | Ticketless passengers risk an open-air ride on a train roof to reach loved ones for the Eid al-Fitr holiday amid crippling traffic throughout the area. *(Muhammad Mostafigur Rahman)*

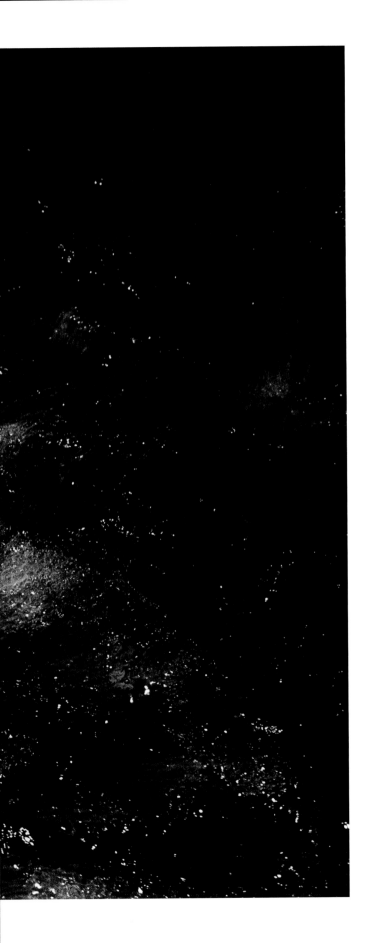

LEFT: **DANUM VALLEY, BORNEO** | A wild king cobra lurches from stream water, announcing it's ready to strike with poised stance, flared hood, and terrifying hiss. *(Mattias Klum)*

FOLLOWING PAGES: **KOLMANSKOP, NAMIBIA** | Desert sands flood dilapidated buildings in a former diamond mining town—once among the world's wealthiest—whose riches were largely depleted by the 1930s. *(Alex Treadway)*

CHENGDU, CHINA | Water gushes into an underwater garage, making a cascade of the stairwell while a resident races toward the bottom during a devastating rainy season. *(China Daily CDIC)*

96

ALL THE MOST POWERFUL EMOTIONS
COME FROM CHAOS—FEAR,
ANGER, LOVE—ESPECIALLY LOVE.
LOVE IS CHAOS ITSELF.

———————————

KIRSTEN MILLER

SAN MIGUEL DE ALLENDE, MEXICO I Ready to move, a folk dancer whirls her skirt
into a halo of green on a cobblestone street. *(Raul Touzon)*

LONDON, ENGLAND | Hundreds of butane lighters salvaged from Hong Kong beaches over three years, then layered into an intergalactic-looking composite image, underscore the world's pollution problem. *(Mandy Barker)*

**ANTARCTICA | ** Plump sea stars cluster in a feeding frenzy deep beneath the frozen continent, where an astounding menagerie of exotic creatures thrives. *(Paul Nicklen)*

LUANGWA VALLEY, ZAMBIA | In a clash of titans, territorial hippos fight in the Luangwa River, leveraging colossal body weight, jaws that can stretch up to four feet wide, and tusk-like teeth. *(Frans Lanting)*

RIGHT: **FUKUSHIMA, JAPAN** I Clad in loincloths, worshippers ascend a rope to the ceiling of an ancient temple in Yanaizu, honoring rites of the Nanokado Hadaka-mairi festival for good luck. *(Teruo Araya)*

PREVIOUS PAGES: **TRACY ARM–FORDS TERROR WILDERNESS, ALASKA** I South Sawyer Glacier's jagged ice glows topaz above the surface of Tracy Arm, where it's flanked by sheer granite. *(Michael Nolan)*

BRITISH COLUMBIA, CANADA I Long-neglected automobiles
appear to melt into the earth as moss and forest enfold them
on the Gulf Islands. *(Pete Ryan)*

VASHON ISLAND, WASHINGTON | As if swallowed up, a bike is pinned to a tree by bark that has grown around it in an intentional design known as arborsculpture. *(Janet Horton)*

SABANA DE TORRES, COLOMBIA | A young jaguar rescued from the underground pet trade glares from his enclosure at the Cabildo Verde nature reserve. *(Steve Winter)*

LEFT: **ALGODONES DUNES, CALIFORNIA** | Off-road vehicles zoom up and down the sand dunes at Glamis, with hundreds of headlights trailing like incandescent ribbons. (*Gerd Ludwig*)

PREVIOUS PAGES: **DES MOINES, IOWA** | Stuntman Gregory "Dr. Danger" Carpenter performs the Suicide Car Jump, bounding from a flaming ramp into a four-car pile—a repeat act that's required multiple hospital trips. (*Joel Sartore*)

RIGHT: **JACKSON HOLE, WYOMING** | A testosterone-fueled face-off intensifies as dueling bulls lock antlers, each making his bid for mating rights at the National Elk Refuge. (*Charlie Hamilton James*)

PAGE 116: **AMSTERDAM, NETHERLANDS** | A water bullet punctures a glass ornament, fracturing the fragile sphere as it explodes. (*Maarten Wouters*)

PAGE 117: **GLASGOW, SCOTLAND** | Concertgoers bathed in blue light raise a hand to buoy the air bubble carrying American music artist Diplo across crowds at a show at 02 Academy Glasgow. (*Ross Gilmore*)

117

SURPRISE

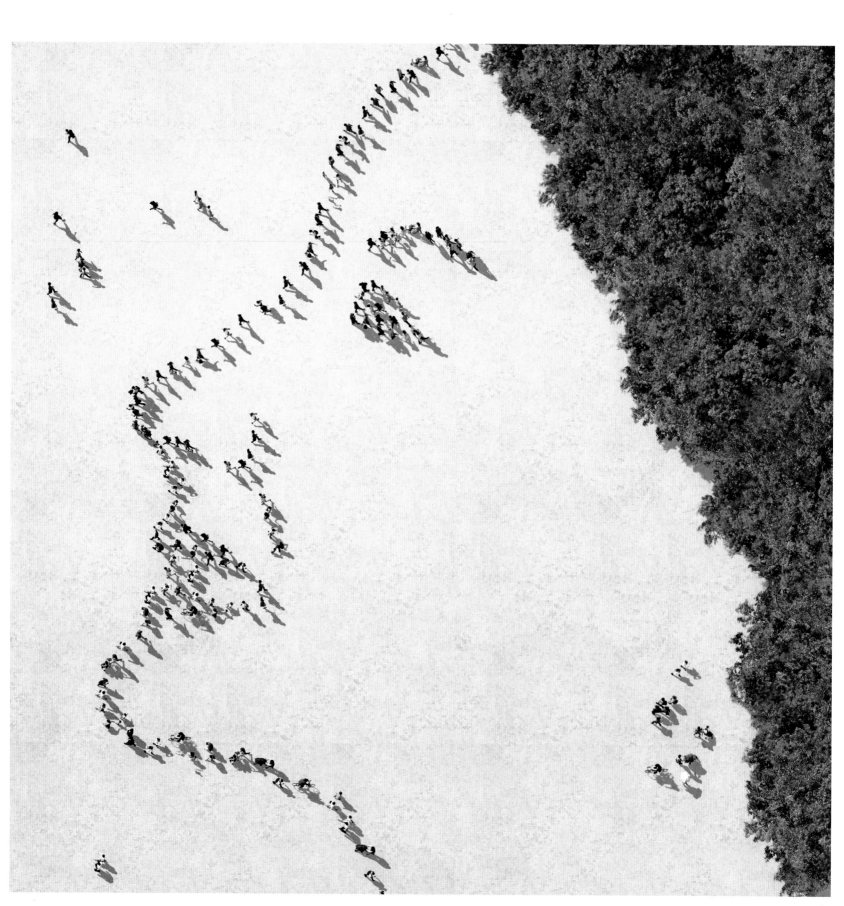

GLIMPSING THE UNEXPECTED

Some photographs surprise us. They reveal sights and scenes, glancing coincidences that strike us as out of the ordinary. Perhaps the photographer was at the right place at the right time and captured the moment: the shy fox against the city skyline, the green lizard skipping across the water, the skateboarder aloft, a beluga's exhalation.

Sometimes surprise arises out of juxtaposition: brilliant fireworks flash-framed by a monumental archway; the ritual seriousness of tribal regalia burst by bubble gum. At other times, though, surprise comes simply by the precious opportunity to see what was always there. Larval scorpions, colorless and vulnerable, throng their venomous mother. A parrotfish smiles, teeth perfect for coral nibbling but comic to our eyes. Rajasthani rugs or Tibetan dwellings form intricate patchworks seen only from on high.

Surprises shock, amuse, and entertain. They make you look—and look again. They can bring a start, a shiver of discomfort, or they can bring a smile—and we're always the better for it, primed to look for more.

OPPOSITE: **JAPAN** | Beachgoers become art when they assemble into an elegant female silhouette cast against smooth sand. *(Hiroshi Watanabe)*

PREVIOUS PAGES: **SAN LUIS OBISPO, CALIFORNIA** | An eruption of spring wildflowers transforms grasslands at Carrizo Plain National Monument into mottled beauty. *(Tim Fitzharris)*

THE HAGUE, NETHERLANDS | Visitors at the miniature city of Madurodam top the skyline as they tread carefully past downscaled replicas of renowned Dutch landmarks. *(David R. Frazier Photolibrary)*

LEFT: **NEW BRITAIN ISLAND, PAPUA NEW GUINEA** | A North American Mitchell B-25H bomber abandoned near scenic Kimbe Bay is a stark reminder of World War II. *(David Doubilet)*

FOLLOWING PAGES: **HONSHU, JAPAN** | A yellow clown goby peers through the entrance of its corroded soda-can home in the Pacific waters off the Izu Peninsula. *(Brian Skerry)*

EVENTUALLY, ALL THINGS
MERGE INTO ONE, AND
A RIVER RUNS THROUGH IT.

———

NORMAN MACLEAN

BAJA CALIFORNIA, MEXICO | Dried riverbeds leave treelike etchings in the Baja California desert. *(Adriana Franco)*

HONG KONG, CHINA | A storefront ad's eye-catching acrobatics frame a passing pedestrian in the retail haven of Kowloon. *(Tino Soriano)*

130

GARZÊ TIBETAN AUTONOMOUS PREFECTURE, CHINA |
Arranged skulls make a mesmerizing tessellation on a shrine at
Larung Gar, an academy and monastery said to be the largest
center of Tibetan Buddhist learning. *(Kampee Patisena)*

GIRONA, SPAIN | Boys take a breather from the yearly Dance of Death performance, part of the Procession of Verges that represents the life and crucifixion of Jesus Christ. *(Tino Soriano)*

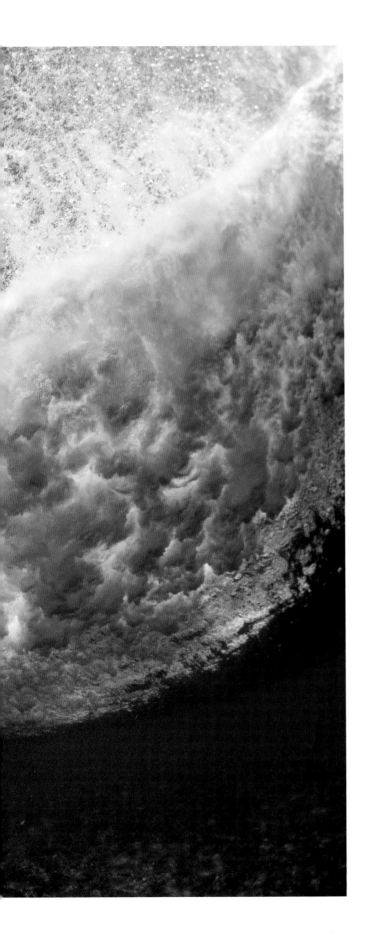

LEFT: **OAHU, HAWAII** I Surfers dodge a wave by diving under it, powering their boards outside the break in the Pacific's legendary waters off the coast of Makaha. *(Paul Nicklen)*

PREVIOUS PAGES: **BRISTOL, ENGLAND** I Wild and urban intersect at the Avon Gorge, where a red fox overlooks the luminous Clifton Suspension Bridge and distant cityscape at night. *(Sam Hobson)*

HONG KONG, CHINA I A stationary cruise ship turned shopping mall keeps business booming amid the ocean of concrete at Whampoa Dock, once one of Asia's busiest shipyards. *(Yann Arthus-Bertrand)*

THE CLEAREST WAY
INTO THE UNIVERSE
IS THROUGH
A FOREST WILDERNESS.

JOHN MUIR

PETRIFIED FOREST NATIONAL PARK, ARIZONA | Sunrise accentuates the natural mineral-based colors
of ancient tree logs that crystallized into almost solid quartz over millions of years. *(George H. H. Huey)*

RIGHT: **RAJASTHAN, INDIA I** A woman walks across the sprawling tapestry made from textiles laid to dry in the sun. *(Callie Chee)*

FOLLOWING PAGES: **EPPING FOREST, ENGLAND I** Aurora, the three-ton, human-operated polar bear puppet that Greenpeace commissioned to protest Arctic drilling, stands ready to march on London streets. *(Kristian Buus)*

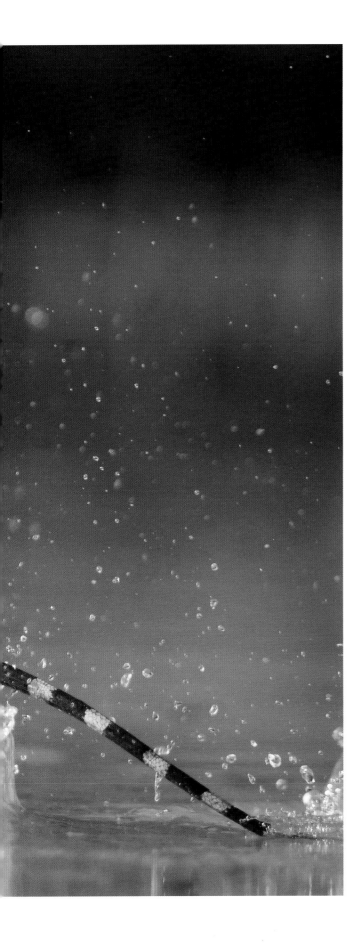

SANTA RITA, COSTA RICA | A green basilisk, also known as a Jesus Christ lizard for its ability to run on water, engages its long toes and agile legs to propel itself at astonishing speed. *(Bence Mate)*

149

RIGHT: **LONDON, ENGLAND** | Workers in neon vests scale a record-size rendering of the royal family as they complete its installation along the South Bank for Queen Elizabeth II's Diamond Jubilee. (John Phillips)

PAGE 148: **ATLANTA, GEORGIA** | The Fantasy Hair competition at the Bronner Bros. International Beauty Show inspires artistry with natural and synthetic locks as medium. (Melissa Golden)

PAGE 149: **PHILADELPHIA, PENNSYLVANIA** | Film extras surround what was then the world's largest piñata before a wrecking ball spills its thousands of pounds of candy. (Andy Newman)

BE GLAD OF LIFE BECAUSE IT
GIVES YOU THE CHANCE TO LOVE
AND TO WORK AND TO PLAY
AND TO LOOK UP AT THE STARS.

———————————————

HENRY VAN DYKE

ST. LOUIS, MISSOURI | A glowing Gateway Arch borders a burst of fireworks honoring the bicentennial anniversary of Lewis and Clark's cross-country odyssey. (*Mike Theiss*)

RIGHT: **SOUTHERN HIGHLANDS, PAPUA NEW GUINEA** | A male King of Saxony vies for female attention by flaunting its lengthy head wires, among other showboating techniques. *(Tim Laman)*

PREVIOUS PAGES: **WUQIAO, CHINA** | Students practice balance and coordination at the Changfa Acrobatic School, one of many training centers that makes the area a hub for aspiring troupers. *(Michael Yamashita)*

LEFT: **SEATTLE, WASHINGTON I** A banner of fog shrouds the city, concealing all but the Space Needle peering above the state ferry cruising the bay below. *(Mara Leite)*

PAGE 160: **SAN FRANCISCO, CALIFORNIA I** A skateboarder soars above the rooftops of an urban neighborhood. *(Chad Riley)*

PAGE 161: **GLACIER NATIONAL PARK, MONTANA I** Lured by exposed salt, a mountain goat maneuvers down a sheer rock wall and reaches for a taste. *(Joel Sartore)*

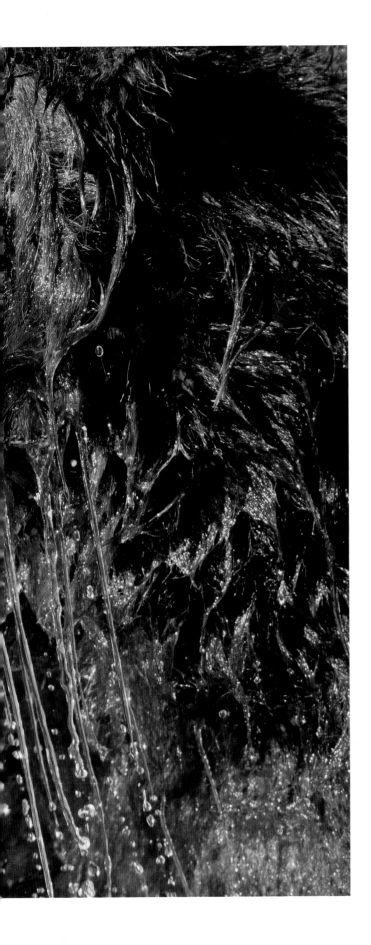

LEFT: **KAMCHATKA, RUSSIA** | A brown bear emerges from the remote waters of Kuril Lake with a thrashing salmon clenched tightly in its jaw. *(Fabrizio Moglia)*

PREVIOUS PAGES: **ALASKA** | Methane bubbling up from a muddy lake bed looks otherworldly entombed in ice. *(Mark Thiessen)*

RIGHT: **OLYMPIC NATIONAL PARK, WASHINGTON** I An ochre sea star, green anemones, and more sea life abound below the surface in the dramatic tidal pools of the wilderness coast. *(Keith Ladzinski)*

FOLLOWING PAGES: **MUYNOQ, UZBEKISTAN** I Rust and sand are all that remain of a fleet that hauled loads of fish to a nearby port before the recession of the Aral Sea. *(Carolyn Drake)*

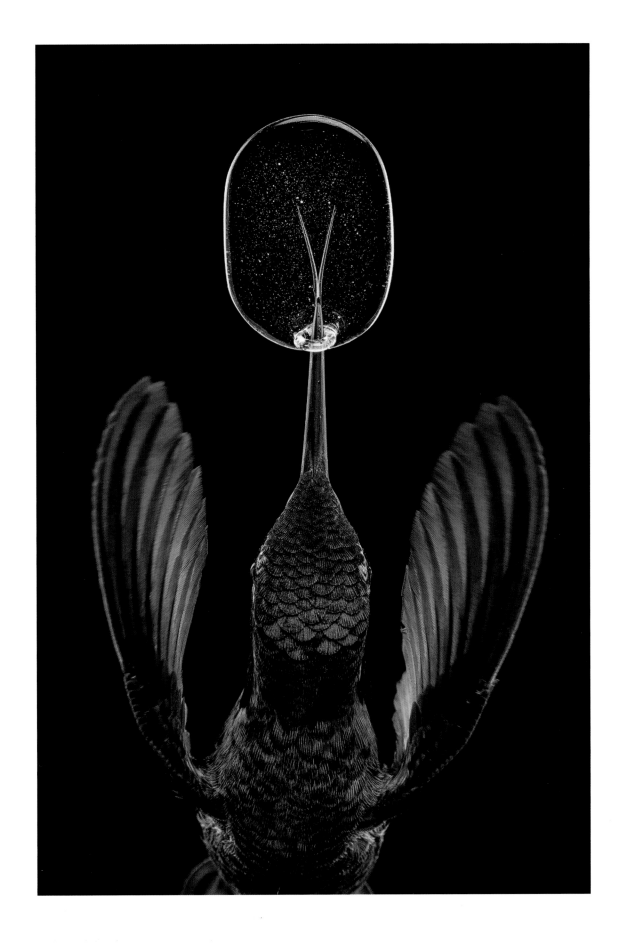

LEFT: **KUMROVEC, CROATIA** | Moss and ferns overtake a lunch counter at the abandoned Josip Broz Tito political school. *(Stefan Baumann)*

PAGE 170: **GOROKA, PAPUA NEW GUINEA** | A girl dressed in tribal regalia blows a chewing gum bubble at a sing-sing, a celebration of Eastern Highlands cultural traditions. *(Jodi Cobb)*

PAGE 171: **UNIVERSITY OF CALIFORNIA RIVERSIDE LAB, CALIFORNIA** | An Anna's hummingbird sips artificial nectar from a glass feeder that reveals its forked tongue, which can make a sipping motion up to 15 times a second. *(Anand Varma)*

FOR THINGS TO REVEAL THEMSELVES
TO US, WE NEED TO BE READY TO
ABANDON OUR VIEWS ABOUT THEM.

THICH NHAT HANH

CHILE | A Chilean scorpion mother ferries her young on her back until they are ready to begin life on their own. *(Alex Hyde)*

LEFT: **MONCTON, CANADA | ** More than a ton of wasted plastic is revitalized as a giant turtle representing environmental consciousness at a city art festival. *(Bordalo II)*

PREVIOUS PAGES: **AOMORI PREFECTURE, JAPAN | ** Nine plant varieties cultivated into a panoramic portrait of an Edo-era courtesan animate a rice paddy in the summer. *(JTB Photo)*

NAIROBI, KENYA | A resident Rothschild's giraffe's craned head superimposes a six-year-old girl's as she offers a treat of bran pellets and molasses at Giraffe Manor in Lang'ata. *(Robin Moore)*

QUEENSLAND, AUSTRALIA | At Killarney Glen, a crystalline waterfall
feeds a heart-shaped rock pool secluded by bush and rain forest. *(Bob Charlton)*

**PAGE, ARIZONA | ** Sunlight sets the contours aglow in a heart-shaped opening of sandstone in Lower Antelope Canyon. *(Sandy L. Kirkner)*

LEFT: **PASIR RIS PARK, SINGAPORE** | A crow chases a trespassing Buffy Fish Owl from its territory, mobbing the intruder with the din of his caws. *(Lawrence Chia Boon Oo)*

PREVIOUS PAGES: **CATALONIA, SPAIN** | En route to a summer festival, masked revelers are engulfed in a sea of yellow while they cross a blooming mustard field near Lake Banyoles. *(Tino Soriano)*

RIGHT: **GREAT BARRIER REEF, AUSTRALIA** | A close-up of a bridled parrotfish's mouth mimics a clown's grin with complete upper and lower rows of straight teeth. *(David Doubilet)*

PAGE 190: **WANAKA, NEW ZEALAND** | Early morning light reflects a solitary tree in the glassy waters of Lake Wanaka below the Southern Alps. *(Linda Cutche)*

PAGE 191: **PARIA CANYON–VERMILION CLIFFS WILDERNESS AREA, ARIZONA** | Twin buttes tower above a ruddy landscape of slickrock that the elements sculpted over millions of years. *(Rex Naden)*

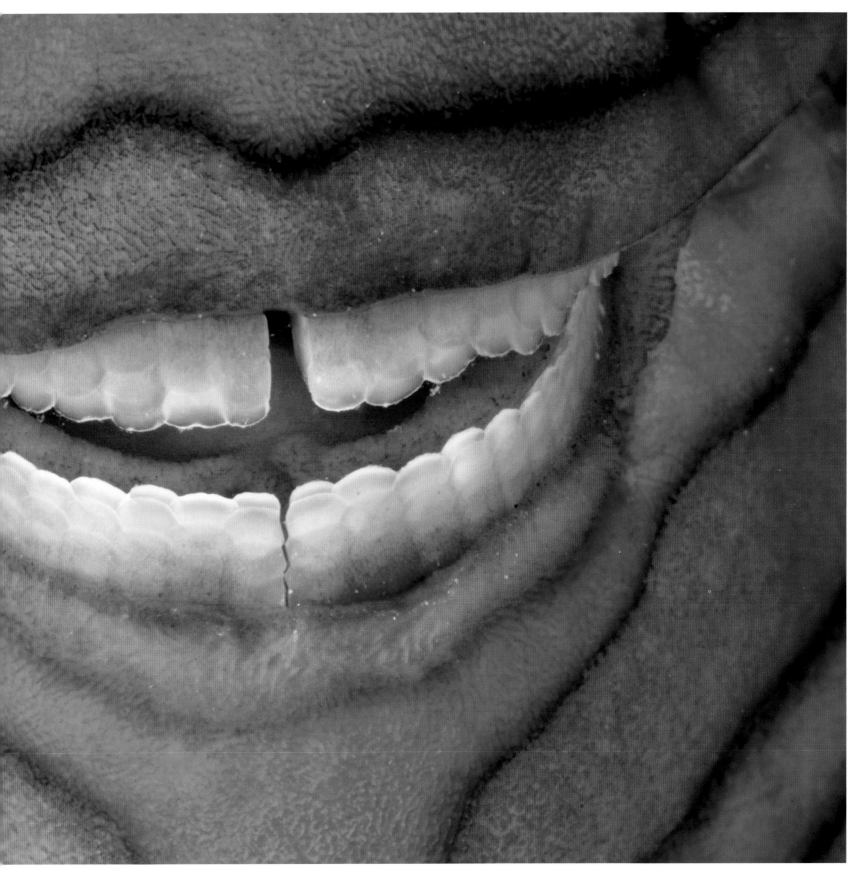

RIGHT: **YOKOHAMA, JAPAN** I Pikachu doubles squeeze onto an elevator during the Pokémon Company's six-day Pikachu Outbreak event, joining droves of gamers in identical yellow costumes. *(Tomohiro Ohsumi)*

PREVIOUS PAGES: **GARZÊ TIBETAN AUTONOMOUS PREFECTURE, CHINA** I A red sea of dwellings for students and disciples surrounds the Tibetan Buddhist academy and monastery at Larung Gar. *(Fei Yang)*

195

JAVA, INDONESIA | Sulfur ignites into a liquidlike blue blaze as it hits the air near a miner in the Kawah Ijen volcanic crater. *(Olivier Grunewald)*

UNEXPECTED INTRUSIONS OF BEAUTY.

THIS IS WHAT LIFE IS.

———————————

SAUL BELLOW

SHIMANE PREFECTURE, JAPAN | A beluga whale in an aquarium blows a bubble ring,
a charming pastime of the massive mammals. *(Hiroya Minakuchi)*

LEFT: **AREQUIPA, PERU** | Novice nuns of the Dominican Order play ball in a shaded corner of Santa Catalina Monastery, a colonial-era convent in the city's historic center. *(Melissa Farlow)*

PREVIOUS PAGES: **TALLINN, ESTONIA** | Ice crowns a throng of wood poles rising above surface at a former seaport. *(Andrei Reinol)*

OSLO, NORWAY ❙ A ski jumper appears imprinted on blue sky as he glides over a built-in ramp, leaning into flight and holding position to perfect style and gain distance. (*Jon Purcell*)

ROSS SEA, ANTARCTICA | In a flurry of bubbles, graceful emperor penguins rocket from frigid waters onto an ice floe. *(Paul Nicklen)*

KYOTO PREFECTURE, JAPAN | Sprinklers mist the historic thatched farmhouses that are preserved in the Miyama countryside during a biannual fire drill of legendary splendor. *(Masaru Yamauchi)*

207

UNIVERSITY OF SCIENCE AND TECHNOLOGY OF CHINA I
Eerily life-like, robot Jia Jia can hold simple conversation and make facial
expressions, heralding a future of cyborg technology. (*Johannes Eisele*)

BEAUTY

A PLEASURE TO BEHOLD

Some photographs unveil the beauty that surrounds us: those rich harmonies of line, shape, symmetry, and color that bring deep pleasure to the soul. We delight in the elegant forms of nature: tree shadows rippling across an expanse of clean, white snow, majestic birds winging over an unpeopled landscape, the unbelievably delicate features of a tiny damselfly.

We attempt to mirror those exultations: colorful houses, intricate costumes, bold theatrical moments when the spirit of creativity shines through, bright and proud. The hushed and hallowed architecture of our houses of worship reflect years of craft and contemplation, the resulting spaces so exquisite that all who enter fall silent with wonder and gratitude.

Perhaps beauty does reside within the beholder, and photographers lend us their keen eyes to find it. We become the tiger, shaking off after a morning dip, or the egret, lifting up out of the bayou. Then again, what's deemed beautiful by one may seem idiosyncratic and odd to another, like shorn poodles or dreadlocked sadhus. Still we marvel, sensing pleasure in the other; we enjoy, sharing their delight.

OPPOSITE: **SHIRAZ, IRAN** | Daylight filters through stained glass in the Nasir al-Mulk Mosque, stamping the window's kaleidoscopic pattern onto a Persian rug in one of many ornate alcoves. *(Walter Bibikow)*

PREVIOUS PAGES: **MAINCY, FRANCE** | Evoking France's *grand siècle* (great century), the Château de Vaux-le-Vicomte blushes with a crimson glow as a semicircle of fireworks arcs across the garden and reflects in the pool below. *(Diane Cook and Len Jenshel)*

RIGHT: **ASTANA, KAZAKHSTAN I** Attended by traditional Kazakh dancers, a bride awaits her formal unveiling after her wedding ceremony in an opulent palace. *(Gerd Ludwig)*

FOLLOWING PAGES: **MECCA, SAUDI ARABIA I** More than two million Muslims prostrate themselves at the Grand Mosque during the hajj, a pilgrimage Muslims must make at least once in their lifetime if physically and financially able. *(REZA)*

BEAUFORT SEA ǀ A polar bear sow and her two young trek on ice after an autumn freeze off Alaska's Arctic coast. *(Steven Kazlowski)*

219

LAPLAND, SWEDEN I Birch tree shadows striate a carpet of snow in Sarek National Park. *(Orsolya Haarberg)*

ALKMAAR, NETHERLANDS | Tulips bloom in bright bands of color with verdant grass fringing at the height of flower viewing in the Dutch countryside. *(Hollandluchtfoto)*

KINSHASA, DEMOCRATIC REPUBLIC OF CONGO I Suavely dressed members of the Société des Ambianceurs et des Personnes Élégantes— or *sapeurs*—model their clothing shop's style and spirit of economic aspiration. *(Per-Anders Pettersson)*

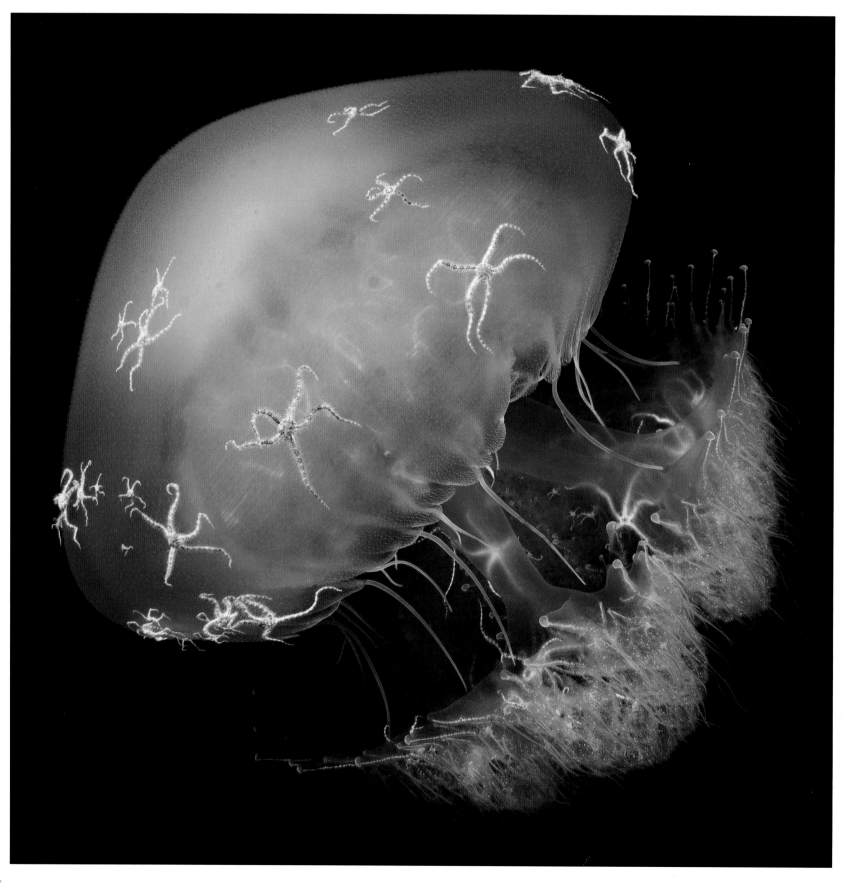

THOSE WHO CONTEMPLATE
THE BEAUTY OF THE EARTH
FIND RESERVES OF STRENGTH
THAT WILL ENDURE AS LONG
AS LIFE LASTS.

————————

RACHEL CARSON

MOZAMBIQUE I Brittle sea stars cleave to a drifting jellyfish like crown jewels on its translucent bell. *(Andrea Marshall)*

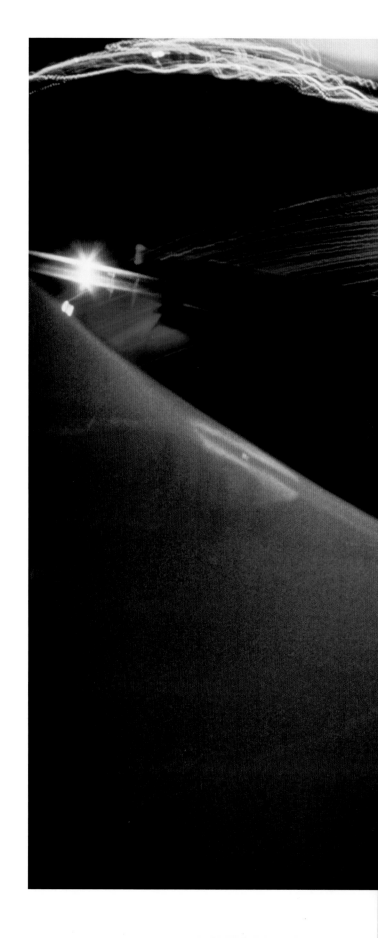

RIGHT: **PALMDALE, CALIFORNIA** | A time exposure by a remotely operated camera captures city and runway lights in electric beams of color from a jetliner's tail. *(Bruce Dale)*

PREVIOUS PAGES: **QUITO, ECUADOR** | A sumptuous nave stretches before the intricately carved wood altarpiece at the center of La Compañía Jesuit cathedral, a baroque vestige fusing European and indigenous art. *(Steve Allen)*

LEFT: **SHAANXI PROVINCE, CHINA** I A harrowing trail of wood planks and carved stone leads to the Chess Pavilion nested on Hua Shan's sloping ridgeline. *(Andrew Suryono)*

PAGE 230: **PALEONTOLOGICAL MUSEUM OF LIAONING, CHINA** I The Silkie—a bantam chicken breed—woos onlookers with its Mohawk-like crest, slate blue skin, and namesake soft plumage, which lacks barbicels, the small hooks that typically hold contour feathers together. *(Robert Clark)*

PAGE 231: **SIBERIA, RUSSIA** I A Nenet woman finds warmth in a hood of reindeer fur. The Nenet depend on reindeer herds for food, clothing, tools, and transportation as they migrate across the Yamal Peninsula tundra. *(Alessandra Meniconzi)*

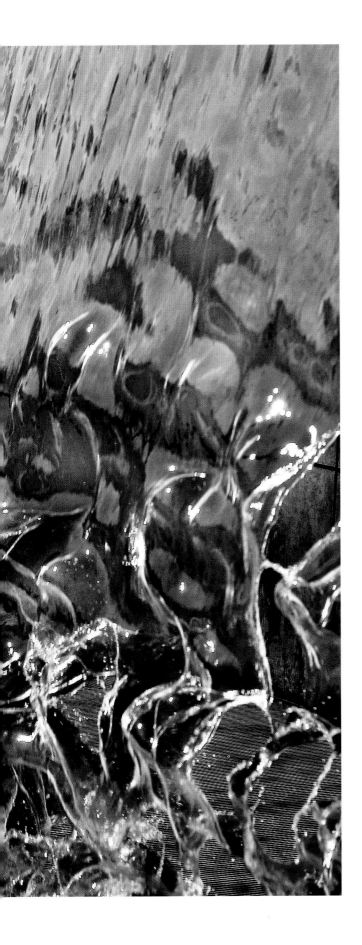

LEFT: **WASHINGTON, D.C.** | A 12-year-old boy splashes through a wall of fountain water in a pool at Yards Park, a recreational area along the Anacostia River. *(Michael S. Williamson)*

PREVIOUS PAGES: **COUSINS ROCK, GALÁPAGOS ISLANDS** | In search of a meal, a Galápagos sea lion tunnels through a school of salema that has parted into a shimmering ring. *(David Doubilet)*

237

PARIA CANYON–VERMILION CLIFFS WILDERNESS AREA, ARIZONA I
A secluded pool of rainwater mirrors the legendary Wave formation,
strata of Navajo sandstone that calcified from primordial sand dunes in
Coyote Buttes North. *(Nicholas Roemmelt)*

EVERYTHING HAS BEAUTY,
BUT NOT EVERYONE SEES IT.

CONFUCIUS

OPPOSITE: **SOMERSET, NEW JERSEY** | A poodle's coat is dyed, fluffed, and cut into an Alaska scene featuring a fish in water and a hunting eagle at an Intergroom styling contest. *(Ren Netherland)*

FOLLOWING PAGES: **ANDALUCIA, SPAIN** | Flamingos fly over amber marshland, their graceful figures and telltale pinks popping against the dark of a deep riverbed at sunset. *(Aya Okawa)*

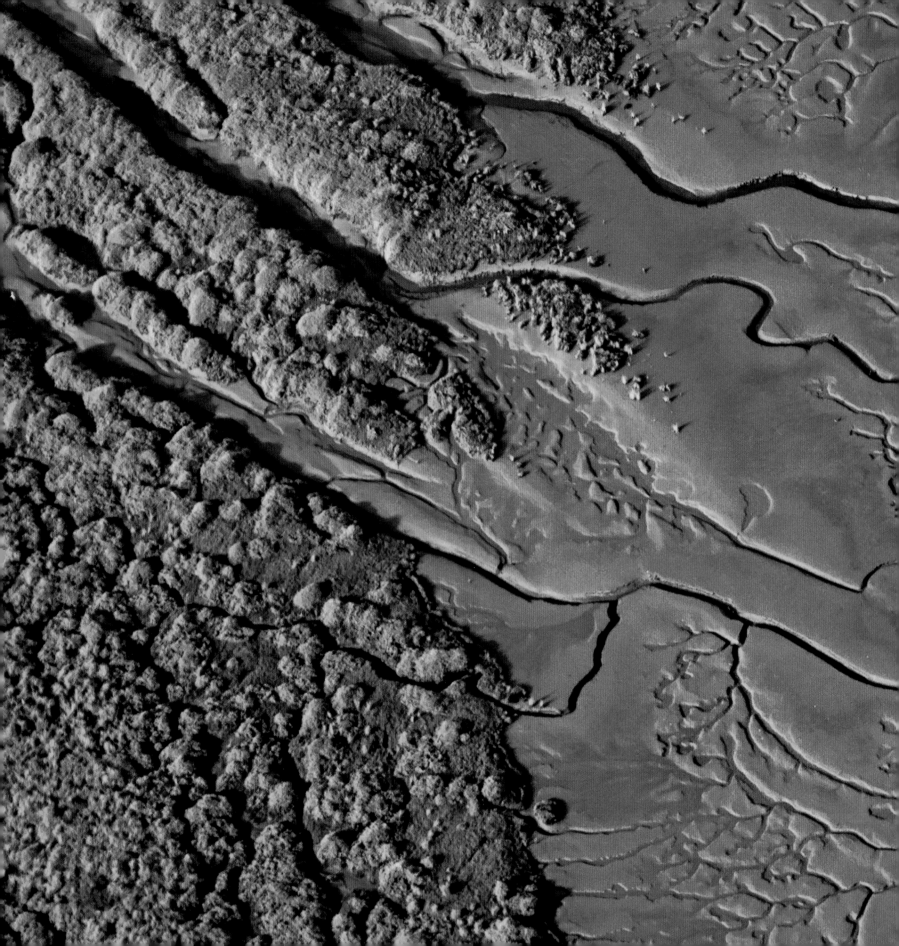

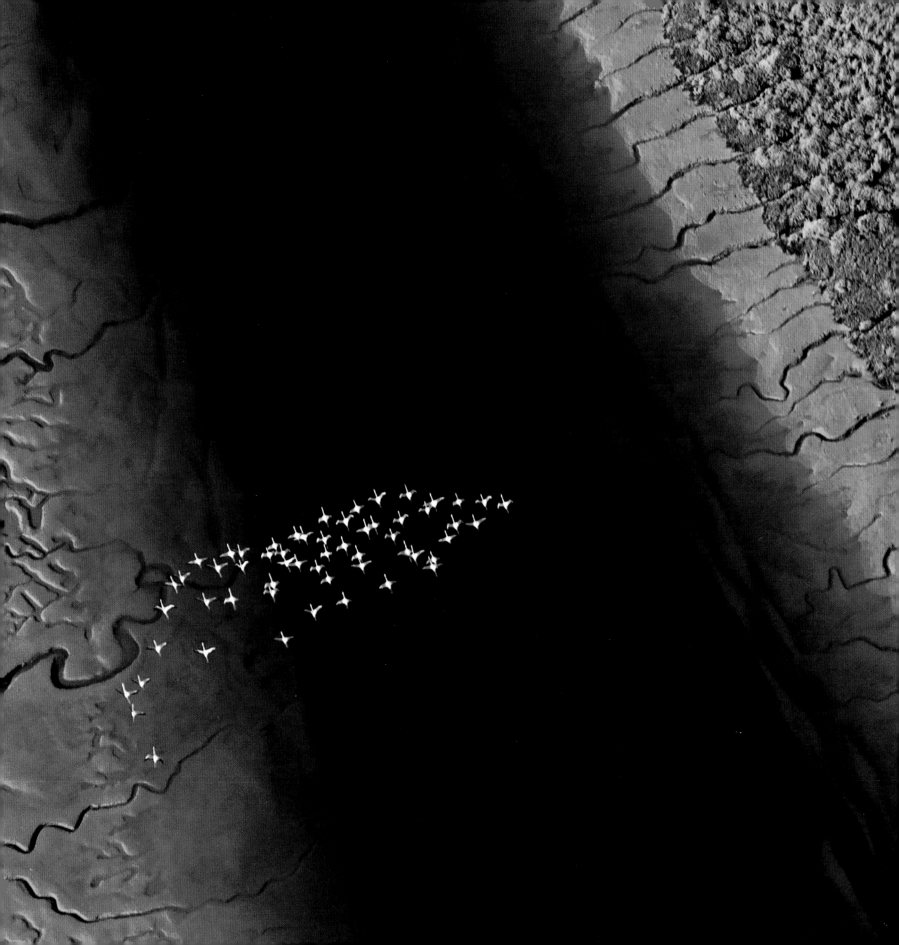

NICOSIA, CYPRUS I A pair of praying mantises pose in an elegant defensive posture: torsos raised, forelegs reaching high and wide, and wings flashing. *(Hasan Baglar)*

ALLAHABAD, INDIA | A Hindu holy man, or *naga* sadhu, rides toward the river to bathe—a ritual of purification from sin—during one of the Kumbh Mela festivals held every 12 years. *(Eric Lafforgue)*

HOUSTON, TEXAS I The diamond, silver, and gold Empress Josephine Tiara sits on display at the Museum of Natural Science. It was designed by August Holmström for the House of Fabergé in the 1890s and is only 5.2 inches wide. *(Heritage Images)*

SVALBARD, NORWAY | A parked walrus flicks his iconic tusks. The enormous, arcing canines can help the marine mammal haul its body from the icy waters of the Bellsund sound. *(Paul Nicklen)*

RIGHT: **ST. MARTINVILLE, LOUISIANA** | An egret spreads its magnificent white wings and takes flight before an audience of waterbirds on a foggy morning at Lake Martin in the Cypress Island Preserve. *(Zeralda La Grange)*

PREVIOUS PAGES: **JOO CHIAT, SINGAPORE** | A row of colonial shophouses painted in pastel tones preserves the classical facades, shuttered windows, and ornate plasterwork that high-rises have largely displaced in the area. *(Mohsin Abrar)*

LEFT: **SICHUAN PROVINCE, CHINA** | Dancers at Shechen monastery perform for a festival commemorating the epic of King Gesar, the ancient hero who conquers evil and stars in generations of Tibetan folklore. *(Michael Yamashita)*

PAGE 256: **CÓRDOBA, SPAIN** | Vistas of columns and arches, carved marble, elaborate mosaics: Striking Islamic and Christian touches layer the medieval Mezquita of Córdoba. *(Michele Falzone)*

PAGE 257: **ÁGUEDA, PORTUGAL** | Rows of parasols dangling on rooftop cables shade a street from the summer sun as part of the Umbrella Sky Project at the AgitÁgueda art festival. *(Francisco Goncalves)*

THERE IS ONE SPECTACLE
GRANDER THAN THE SEA,
THAT IS THE SKY;
THERE IS ONE SPECTACLE
GRANDER THAN THE SKY,
THAT IS THE INTERIOR
OF THE SOUL.

———————

VICTOR HUGO

OPPOSITE: **OMO VALLEY, ETHIOPIA** | Displaying his body paint and headwear, a boy takes pride in the generations-old tribal traditions that endure in his home village along the Omo River. *(Josef Bürgi)*

PREVIOUS PAGES: **PATAGONIA, CHILE** | Waves lapping against calcium carbonate eroded the Marble Caves into sinuous aquamarine curves in Lake General Carrera. *(Clane Gessel)*

TOKUSHIMA PREFECTURE, JAPAN | A bridge of woven wisteria vines and wood planks, thought to have been constructed by 12th-century Heike warriors, spans the ravine of the Iya River. *(Macduff Everton)*

LEFT: **CHIANG RAI, THAILAND** I The colorless facade of Wat Rong Khun, or the White Temple, signifies purity, while its elaborate engravings blend Buddhist imagery and pop culture into more complex symbolism. *(C. Camarena)*

PAGE 266: **TACOMA, WASHINGTON** I Teal eyespots tinged with gold and green adorn the sweeping, majestic feather trains that can make up more than half of a peacock's body length. *(Karine Aigner)*

PAGE 267: **LOFOTEN, NORWAY** I Northern lights appear in a plume of green that flickers above a frozen landscape in the Arctic Circle. *(Christian Ringer)*

265

LEFT: **COUNTY ANTRIM, NORTHERN IRELAND** | Sunlight fades from the Causeway Coast's tiers of basalt columns, which are so dramatic they've inspired legends of giants who followed the "stepping-stones" to Scotland. *(Francesco Vaninetti)*

PREVIOUS PAGES: **ST. PETERSBURG, FLORIDA** | Seven young ballerinas rest backstage after portraying fairies for a recital at the Mahaffey Theater. *(Evelyn Reinson)*

**ISFAHAN, IRAN | ** Meticulous handiwork makes for enchanting designs
on the Persian carpets sold at the sprawling Isfahan Bazaar. *(Jason Edwards)*

NORWAY | Using a small bottle, an artist dispenses table salt along the precise contours of a mandala that will take days to complete. *(Dino Tomic)*

VIENTIANE, LAOS I A friend embraces a deaf boy with heterochromia (different-colored eyes) at a rehabilitation center that aids children with congenital disorders. (John Brown)

RIGHT: **FLORENCE, ITALY** I Visitors at the Galleria dell'Accademia peer up at Michelangelo's "David," a 17-foot-tall masterpiece carved from a single block of marble more than 500 years ago. *(Paolo Woods)*

PREVIOUS PAGES: **ZAMBIA** I Marching in perfect single file, a pride of lions takes advantage of tire tracks to prowl through swaths of golden grass. *(Torie Hilley)*

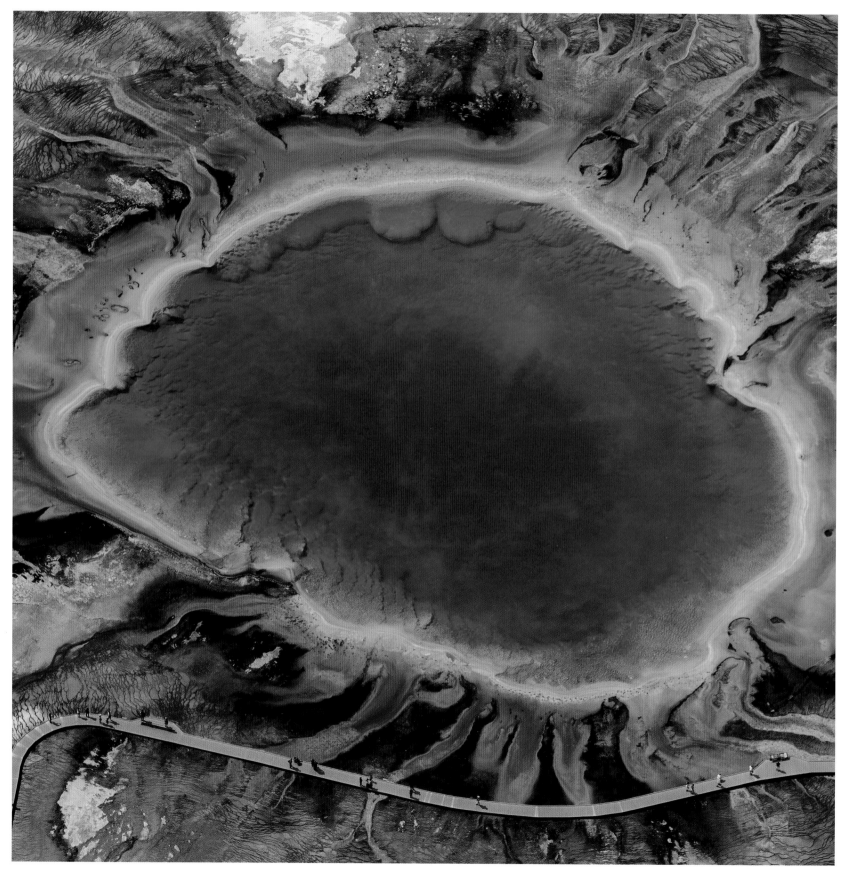

ALL IN THE EYE OF THE BEHOLDER—
SOME OF THE MOST DESTRUCTIVE FORCES
IN THE WORLD CAN ALSO HAVE
THE POWER OF BEAUTY.

————————————

MARTIN R. LEMIEUX

OPPOSITE: **YELLOWSTONE NATIONAL PARK, WYOMING** | Hot water pools into iridescent rings of color at
Grand Prismatic Spring, each tinted by thermophilic bacteria, minerals, and temperature gradients. *(Michael Yamashita)*

PAGE 282: **MANÚ NATIONAL PARK, PERU** | A pet saddleback tamarin clings to a Matsigenka girl's head
as she takes a dip in the Yomibato River, deep in a protected rain forest. *(Charlie Hamilton James)*

PAGE 283: **LONDON, ENGLAND** | A Chinese water dragon draped across a woman's Mohawk melds
into a statuesque silhouette of singular beauty. *(Tim Flach)*

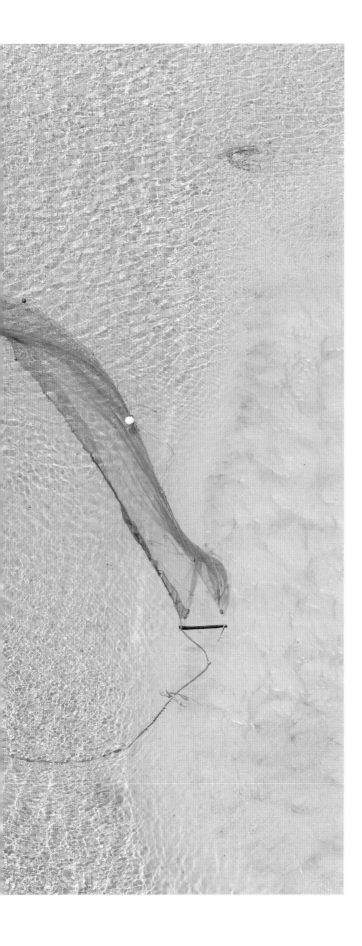

LEFT: **BENGUERRA, MOZAMBIQUE** | Locals fish the shallows between islands at low tide in the Bazaruto Archipelago, unfurling turquoise nets that the crew will later pull in by hand. *(George Steinmetz)*

PREVIOUS PAGES: **CHIANG MAI, THAILAND** | Paper lanterns saturate the night sky in a constellation of orange candlelight, emblems of celebrants' wishes at the Yi Peng festival. *(Weerakarn Satitniramai)*

287

RIGHT: **STUTTGART, GERMANY** | Readers linger in the "heart" of a modern public library, a sunlit atrium wrapped with walls of books and sleek promenades adjoined by central staircases. *(Norbert Fritz)*

PAGE 288: **LUZZARA, ITALY** | Mounted on the sides of its head, the damselfly's globular blue eyes and their fine honeycomb of photoreceptor cells allow it to see all around. *(Alberto Ghizzi Panizza)*

PAGE 289: **LYON, FRANCE** | A psychedelic play of lights accentuates architectural details of the historic St. Jean Cathedral in Yves Moreaux's "Color or Not" installation at the Festival of Lights. *(Pierre Jacques)*

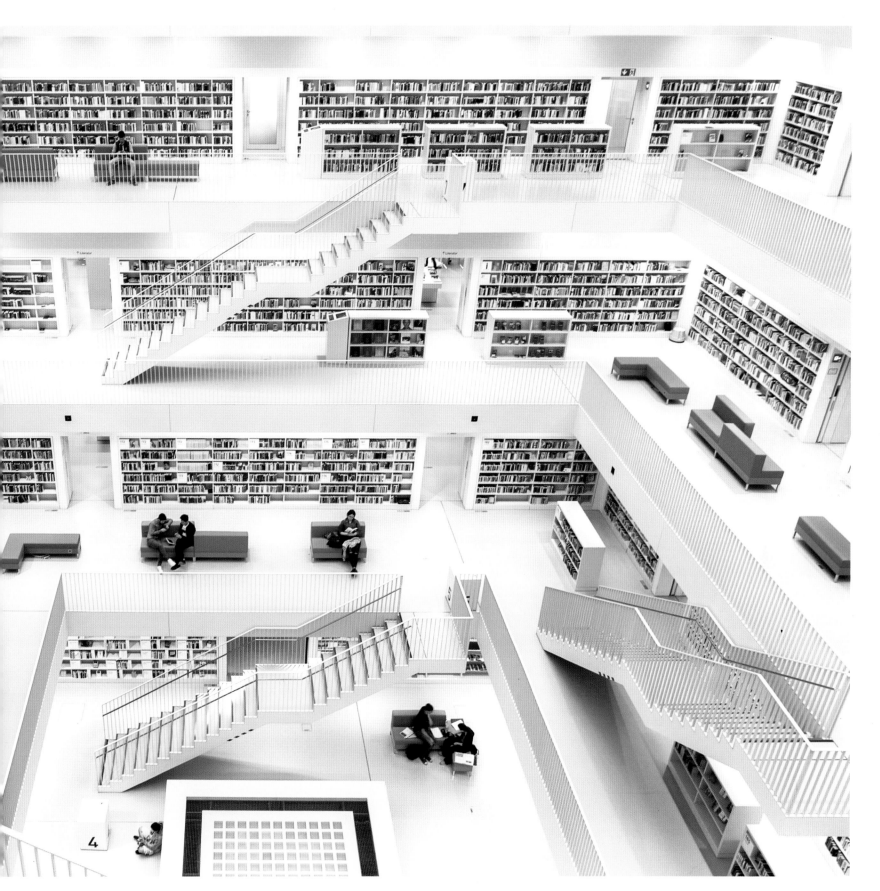

RIGHT: **ARU ISLANDS, INDONESIA** | A greater bird of paradise lifts his wings in a grand flash of feathers whose remarkable shapes, textures, and colors keep him competitive in courtship. *(Tim Laman)*

PREVIOUS PAGES: **XINJIANG PROVINCE, CHINA** | Tajik children huddle together to review notes on a chilly morning before school opens in a Pamir mountain village. *(Michael Yamashita)*

IF THE PATH BE BEAUTIFUL,

LET US NOT ASK

WHERE IT LEADS.

———————————

ANATOLE FRANCE

ZHANGJIAJIE, CHINA | Heaven-Linking Avenue snakes up Tianmen Mountain, bending 99 times along the way in a nod to Chinese numerology: Nine represents good fortune and eternity. *(Oleksiy Maksymenko Photography)*

CHONBURI PROVINCE, THAILAND I An Indochinese tigress—
an endangered species—shakes herself dry after a swim at the
Khao Kheow Open Zoo. *(Ashley Vincent)*

LEFT: **GOJAL, PAKISTAN** | In the village of Zood Khun, family members of a soon-to-be married bride pose for a selfie before the festivities begin. *(Matthieu Paley)*

PREVIOUS PAGES: **ARCTIC BAY, CANADA** | Sheets of ice dwarf a rarely seen pod of narwhals navigating the breaks for their brief surface time. *(Paul Nicklen)*

SUGAR BEACH, TORONTO, CANADA | The underside of a bench
curves into a pinwheel of slats and sunlight. *(Peter Crock)*

WARSAW, POLAND I A worn staircase coils into darkness with a strand of coral railing tracing the outline. *(James Kerwin)*

305

HANOI, VIETNAM | Dyed incense surrounds a worker in cherry red bundles set out to dry at the Quang Phu Cau commune. *(Tran Tuan Viet)*

AWE

INSIGHT INTO THE INEFFABLE

Some photographs leave us speechless and in awe. They can have that power. They can remind us of immensity and the force of mysteries beyond human understanding. As the old saying has it, photographs can say so much more than our words will ever contain.

Meditate upon a vast landscape of solitude and silence. Peer deeply into the intricacies of life inside a scallop's shell. Let the dancing lasers of Burning Man, or the cold, blue lights of an ice cave, or the fleeting flickers of rising mayflies shine for a moment in your own imagination. Grand or minuscule, natural or human-made, these are moments of wonder captured forever.

We gaze with awe on the wonders of nature—a multitude of monarch butterflies, magnificent cloud formations, the indescribably deep crimson of a chili pepper harvest. Human accomplishments can leave us awestruck, too: military precision, daring horse-manship, balletic flexibility.

This world we live in, with all its imperfections, still has splendors aplenty to see. Hints of chaos, moments of surprise, reflections of beauty, opportunities for awe—spectacles such as these affirm our better selves and remind us to keep eyes and hearts wide open.

OPPOSITE: **VATICAN CITY** | Pope Francis finds quiet on an impromptu visit to the Sistine Chapel after giving his *"Urbi et Orbi"* address to masses on Christmas Day. *(Dave Yoder)*

PREVIOUS PAGES: **KINGDOM OF TONGA, VAVA'U** | A freediver swims through a few of the thousands of fish that have settled in Swallows Cave. *(Marc Henauer)*

ANANDPUR SAHIB, INDIA | A Nihang rider straddles galloping horses in a show of martial prowess at Hola Mohalla, a Sikh festival of parades, mock battles, and devotional worship. *(Jeremy Woodhouse)*

LEFT: **DENGFENG, CHINA** | Martial artists spread into a ribbon of orange along a narrow footpath, practicing Shaolin kung fu against Mount Song's vertiginous cliffs. *(VCG)*

PREVIOUS PAGES: **TYNE AND WEAR, ENGLAND** | Seawater surges into a mountainous peak when a storm roils the surf off the coast of Sunderland. *(Philip Payne)*

LONDON, ENGLAND I Cirque du Soleil performers test the
human figure as they contort themselves into geometric sculpture
on the steps leading to Royal Albert Hall. *(Leon Neal)*

MADRID, SPAIN | A rider arches from his bike in a controlled flip at the X-Fighters freestyle motocross competition held at Las Ventas bullring. *(Evrim Aydin)*

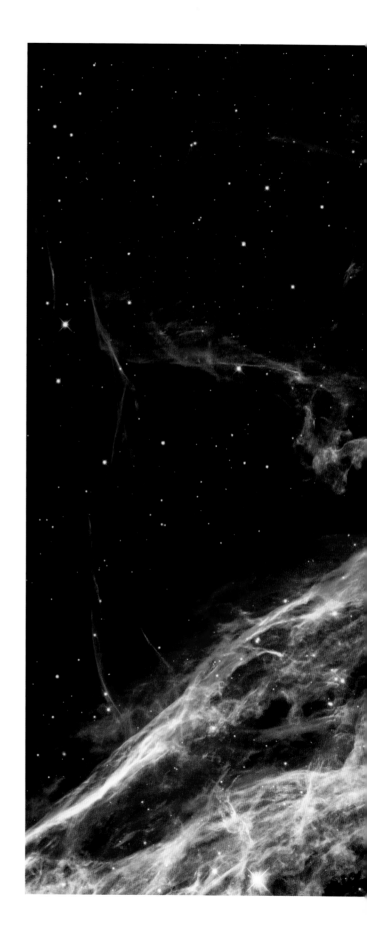

SPACE | Wisps of gas in the Veil Nebula, rendered in opalescent pinks, purples, and yellows by NASA's Hubble Telescope, are remnants of a massive star's explosive end about 8,000 years ago. *(NASA/ESA/ Hubble Heritage Team [STScI/AURA])*

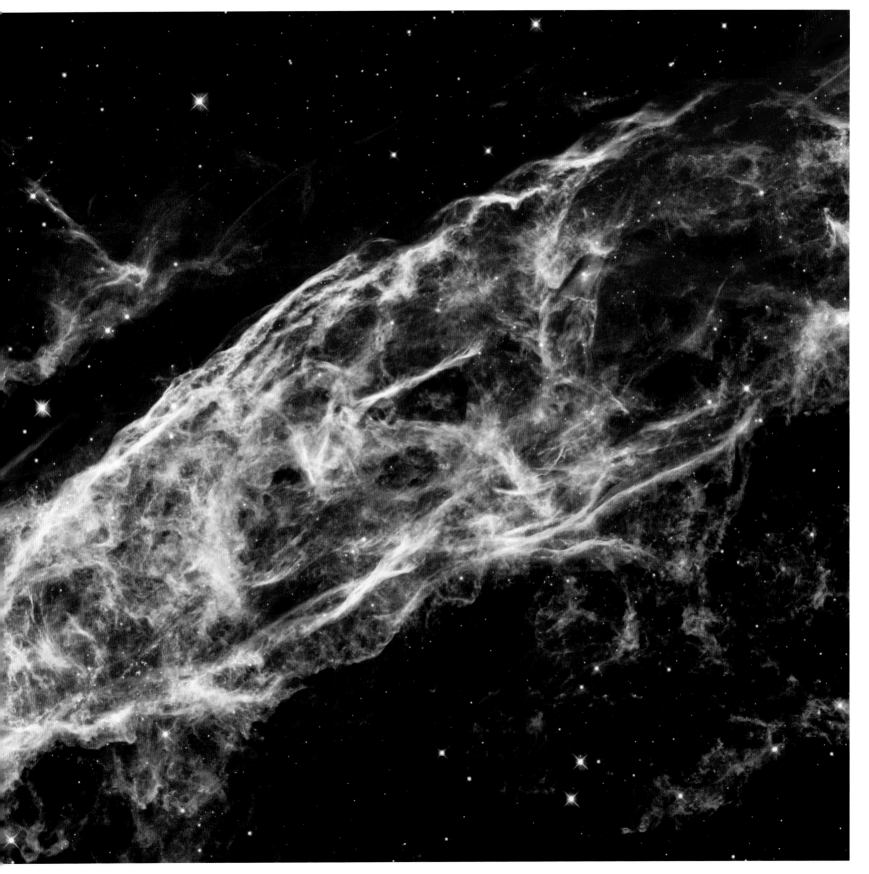

THE UNIVERSE IS FULL

OF MAGICAL THINGS

PATIENTLY WAITING FOR

OUR WITS TO GROW SHARPER.

EDEN PHILLPOTTS

BROOKLYN, NEW YORK | A model's face is masked in gold leaf for a luxurious skin treatment
that makes use of the precious metal's possible beauty benefits. *(Robert Clark)*

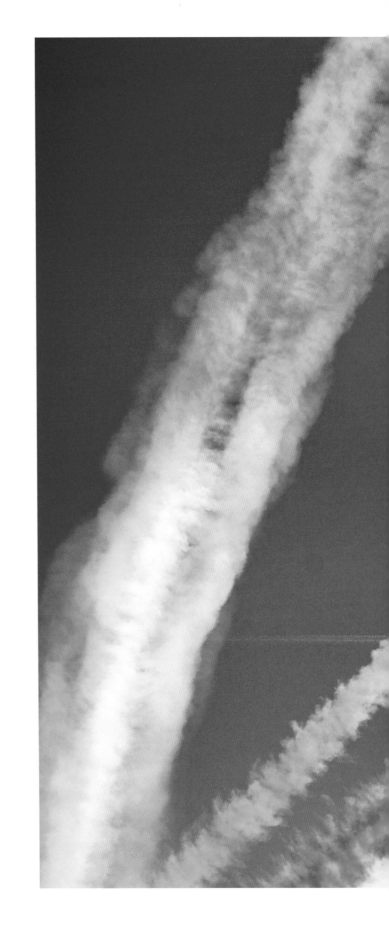

RIGHT: **ALTA BADIA, ITALY** | Italy's special air force unit, Frecce Tricolori, paints the sky with the colors of the country's flag during the FIS Alpine Skiing World Cup. *(Olivier Morin)*

PREVIOUS PAGES: **DHAKA, BANGLADESH** | Prostrate on prayer rugs for Friday Jummah, Muslim congregants at the Baitul Mukarram Mosque align in neat rows checkered with bright outfits. *(Sohel Parvez Haque)*

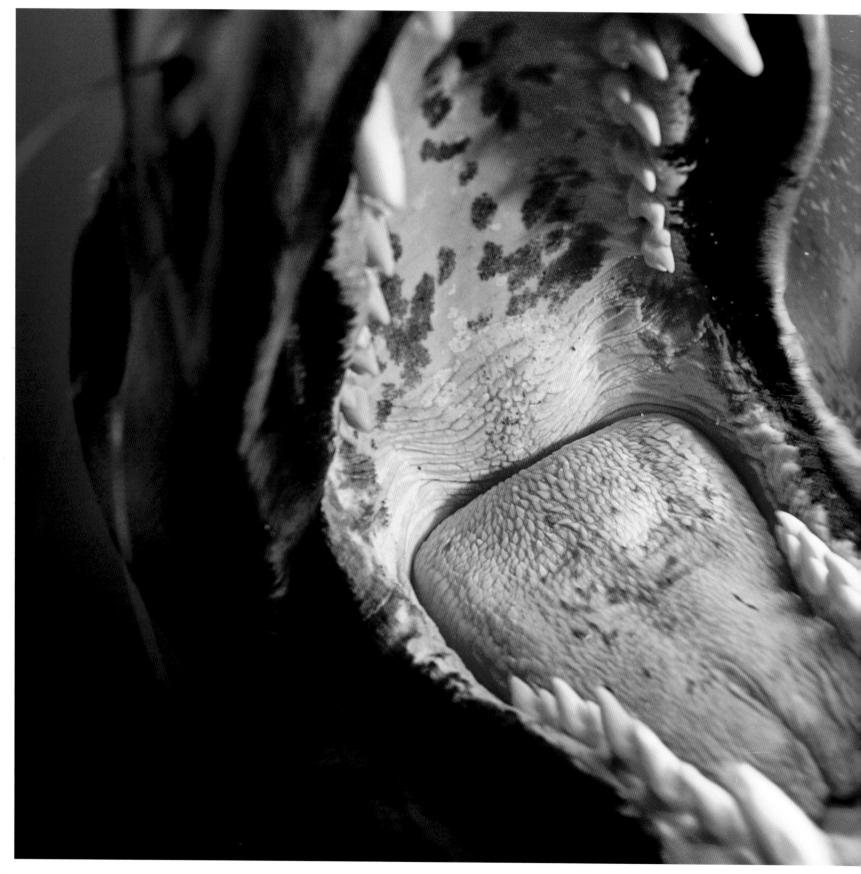

LEFT: **ANTARCTICA** | A leopard seal bares its teeth at a photographer's lens. *(Paul Nicklen)*

PAGE 330: **VIC, SPAIN** | A *castell,* or human tower, rises as *castellers* climb tiers of their huddled teammates to reach their place in the short-lived structure, with a tight net of people buttressing them below. *(Mika-Pekka Markkanen)*

PAGE 331: **MICHOACÁN, MEXICO** | Monarch butterflies cluster into a column of orange on an oyamel fir tree in the Monarch Butterfly Biosphere Reserve after their annual autumnal migration from as far as eastern Canada. *(Medford Taylor)*

329

RIGHT: **SYDNEY, AUSTRALIA** I On a rare daytime outing in Parramatta Park, a gray-headed flying fox skims the water to wet his fur, which he'll lick to get a drink. (*Ofer Levy*)

PREVIOUS PAGES: **GUANGXI ZHUANG AUTONOMOUS REGION, CHINA** I A mountainous landscape unfolds in shaded layers as morning mist meets light. (*Istvan Kadar Photography*)

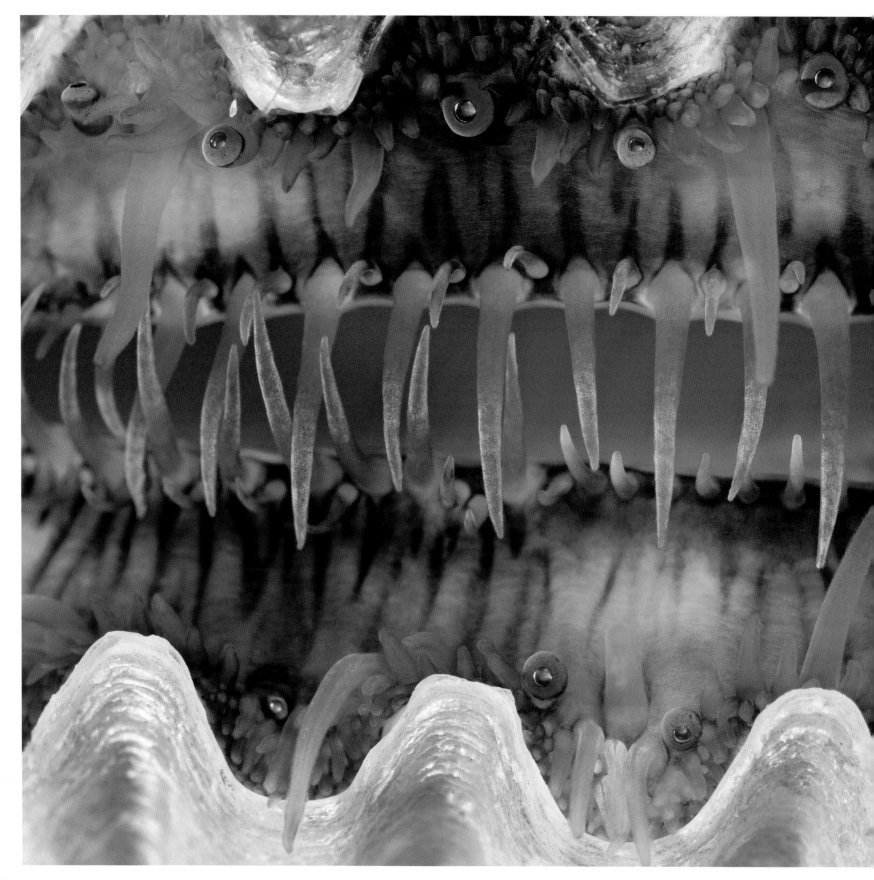

SAN FRANCISCO, CALIFORNIA | A peek between the ridged shells of a mantle of the bay scallop reveals the brilliant blue "eyes" that adorn the mollusk and enable it to sense movement and shadows. *(David Liittschwager)*

IT IS NOT LIGHT THAT IS NEEDED,
BUT FIRE; IT IS NOT THE GENTLE SHOWER,
BUT THUNDER. WE NEED THE STORM,
THE WHIRLWIND, AND THE EARTHQUAKE.

FREDERICK DOUGLASS

OPPOSITE: **SICILY, ITALY** | Seen from a distance, a paroxysm of Mt. Etna takes over the sky. *(Nunzio Santisi)*

FOLLOWING PAGES: **MONTE PIANA, ITALY** | After walking the suspension wire to their hammocks, slackliners— or "slackers"—dangle at dizzying heights amid the Dolomites. *(Sebastian Wahlhuetter)*

338

INSTITUTE OF ZOOLOGY AND ZOOLOGICAL MUSEUM, HAMBURG, GERMAN I
A close-up of a male red bird of paradise's fiery plume spotlights the embellishments
that help attract picky females. *(Robert Clark)*

KIMBE BAY, PAPUA NEW GUINEA | A silvery school of razorfish keeps formation as it darts for cover in the slender branches of a red sea whip. *(David Doubilet)*

BOGRA, BANGLADESH I Laborers pick through thousands
of sun-dried chilies, clearing narrow strips in the red expanse as
they crouch under umbrellas for shade. *(Azim Khan Ronnie)*

LEFT: **LONDON, ENGLAND** I Splendor gleams overhead in Henry VII's Lady Chapel at Westminster Abbey, where a fan-vaulted ceiling with intricately carved pendants crowns the extraordinary feat of architecture. *(Jim Richardson)*

FOLLOWING PAGES: **BLACK ROCK DESERT, NEVADA** I Lasers light the night like a beacon for thousands of partygoers who have flocked to Burning Man's pop-up city for alternative art, culture, and carousing. *(Aaron Huey)*

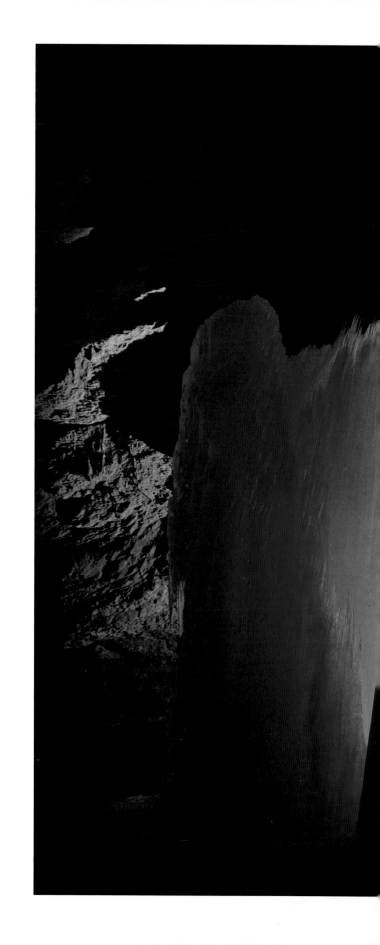

SALZBURG, AUSTRIA | A trekker's profile appears shrunken amid the colossal, blue-toned ice formations in the Eiskogelhöhle cave, high in the Alps' Tennengebirge Range. *(Robbie Shone)*

LEFT: **HUNGARY** | Mayflies swarm the Rába River in a brief mating frenzy that begins at sunset and ends with their deaths, often within hours. *(Imre Potyó)*

PAGE 354: **CARIBOU, MAINE** | A gum-ball cluster of helium balloons carries its pilot over mountainous terrain on the starting leg of a journey that will end in Canada. *(Paul Cyr)*

PAGE 355: **ATLANTA, GEORGIA** | Balloons hold a model's pink hair on end before an art director cuts the carefully sectioned tresses on stage at the Bronner Bros. International Beauty Show. *(Melissa Golden)*

IF THE WORLD COULD REMAIN WITHIN
A FRAME LIKE A PAINTING ON A WALL
THEN I THINK WE'D SEE THE BEAUTY THEN
WE'D STAND STARING IN AWE.

CONOR OBERST

OPPOSITE: **JAKARTA, INDONESIA** I Morning dewdrops ornament the tufted seeds of a
dandelion head atop a curling stem. *(Saefull Regina)*

PREVIOUS PAGES: **DANAKIL DEPRESSION, ETHIOPIA** I The interplay of minerals, gases, and geological activity
renders the alien terrain of the Dallol volcano in multicolor. *(Eric Lafforgue)*

PRINCE WILLIAM SOUND, ALASKA I Kayakers approach
Meares Glacier at its end in the Unakwik Inlet, where a continuous
parade of falling ice pierces the glossy water. *(Ernest Manewal)*

360

LEFT: **BEIJING, CHINA** | Military men in pristine white uniform embody precision as they march in tandem for the National Day of the People's Republic of China. *(Paul Chesley)*

PAGE 364: **TABASCO, MEXICO** | Midges feed on sticky biofilm that drips from the walls of Cueva de Villa Luz, a forbidding limestone cave permeated by a toxic brew of natural gases. *(Mark Thiessen)*

PAGE 365: **KENSINGTON, MARYLAND** | A 17-year-old cicada from Brood X emerges from its nymphal shell with bulging red eyes and ribbed wings that will aid in flight and courtship during its short adult life. *(Darlyne A. Murawski)*

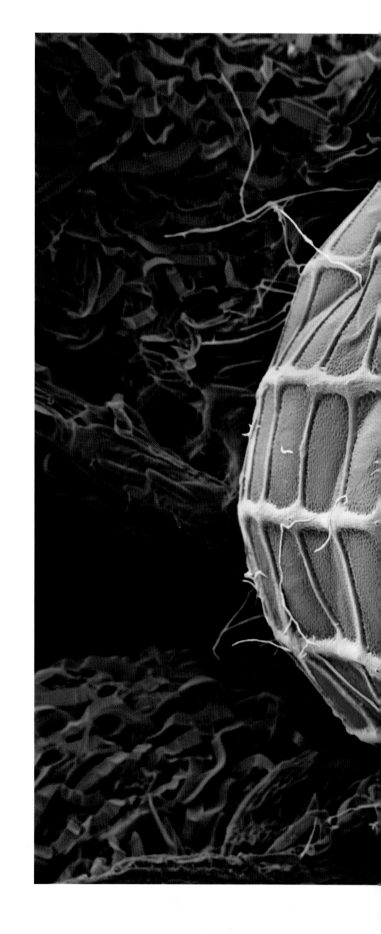

RIGHT: **FHNW SCHOOL OF LIFE SCIENCES, SWITZERLAND** I Shown in exquisite detail by microscope, the tiny orange egg of a zebra longwing butterfly cradles the maturing larva of a future striped-winged beauty. *(Martin Oeggerli)*

PREVIOUS PAGES: **DUBLIN, IRELAND** I A stately procession of bookshelves preserves written treasures below a soaring barrel ceiling in the Long Room of the Old Library at Trinity College. *(Thibaud Poirier)*

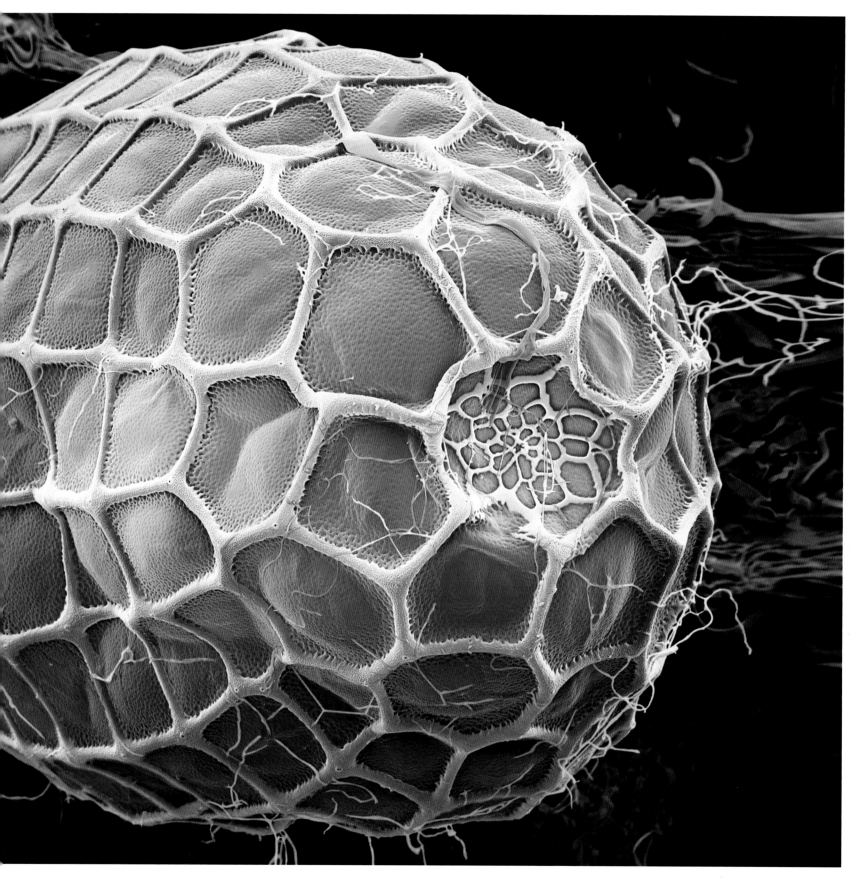

MECCA, SAUDI ARABIA | Muslim pilgrims pour into Mina in broad, river-like lines for the Jamarat—the symbolic stoning of the devil—during the five-day hajj that fills the holy city with worshippers. *(Mustafa Ozer)*

RIGHT: **LESHAN, CHINA** I Carved into the hillside in the eighth century, the world's biggest Buddha remains a transcendent part of the landscape where Buddhism was first established in China. *(Oktay Ortakcioglu)*

FOLLOWING PAGES: **SEELEY LAKE, MONTANA** I The path ahead is treacherous for a firefighter supervisor surveying the scene after a roaring blaze jumped the road. *(Mark Thiessen)*

KIMBE BAY, PAPUA NEW GUINEA | A pagurid hermit crab's purple legs betray its hideout as it inches outward from a coral burrow that tube worms made. *(David Doubilet)*

ARCADIA, CALIFORNIA | Ultraviolet light reveals alien-like colors and otherworldly sparkles on everyday plants and flowers. *(Craig P. Burrows)*

**MIYAZAKI, JAPAN | ** Swimmers crowd the always-temperate, always blue-skied artificial beach in the Seagaia Ocean Dome, formerly one of the world's largest indoor waterparks. *(Martin Parr)*

DWELL ON THE BEAUTY OF LIFE.
WATCH THE STARS,
AND SEE YOURSELF
RUNNING WITH THEM.

———————

MARCUS AURELIUS

LOFOTEN ISLANDS, NORWAY I The dazzling colors of an aurora borealis light up the sky
and reflect in the waters near Reine village. *(Daniel Kordan)*

LEFT: **PENTECOST, VANUATU** I A man jumps from a bamboo tower with bamboo vines around his ankles as part of ritualistic land diving, a rite of passage on the island. *(Michael Runkel)*

FOLLOWING PAGES: **SERENGETI NATIONAL PARK, TANZANIA** I C-Boy, one of two adult male lions in the Vumbi pride, tears into a zebra carcass at dusk after a day of guarding his group's kill. *(Michael Nichols)*

RIGHT: **WULONG DISTRICT, CHINA** I Explorers traverse the Sea of Tranquility, a gentler stretch of the San Wang Dong cave whose known 40-plus miles hold gushing streams, giant stalagmites, and gaping pits. (*Robbie Shone*)

PAGE 386: **CAPE CANAVERAL, FLORIDA** I The SpaceX Falcon 9 rocket streaks a cobalt sky as it launches from NASA's Kennedy Space Center, hauling tons of cargo destined for the International Space Station. (*Bill Ingalls*)

PAGE 387: **MEXICO** I A thrill seeker on a jet-propelled flyboard blasts straight up from the water's surface, demonstrating the air potential of another craze in extreme sports. (*Justin Lewis*)

LEFT: **RIO DE JANEIRO, BRAZIL I** A stand-up paddleboarder catches a premium view as New Year's fireworks paint the horizon in shimmering pinks at Copacabana Beach. *(Mario Tama)*

FOLLOWING PAGES: **MASAI MARA NATIONAL RESERVE, KENYA I** Blue wildebeests rush the bank after surviving the Mara River crossing, a deadly segment of their migration journey. *(Elliott Neep)*

POLAND | A baby enters the world with arms outstretched,
just after midnight. *(Tomasz Solinski)*

YA'AN, CHINA | Visitors press against a window to glimpse an infant panda curled in a caretaker's arms at the Bifengxia Panda Center. *(Ami Vitale)*

LOOK DEEP INTO NATURE,
AND THEN YOU WILL UNDERSTAND
EVERYTHING BETTER.

———————

ALBERT EINSTEIN

NOSY HARA NATIONAL PARK, MADAGASCAR | A fingertip provides a sizable perch for a chameleon species called *Brookesia micra,* one of the smallest vertebrates discovered on Earth yet. *(Christian Ziegler)*

ADDITIONAL CREDITS

ACKNOWLEDGMENTS

Spectacle would not have been possible without the talents of the many photographers featured within these pages and the hard work of the wonderful National Geographic team: photo editors Laura Lakeway and Meredith Wilcox, designer and production design manager Katie Olsen, editorial project manager Allyson Johnson, deputy editor Hilary Black, creative director Melissa Farris, senior editor Susan Tyler Hitchcock, researcher Anne Staub, senior production editor Judith Klein, and countless others who gave their time and talent to this book.

Since 1888, the National Geographic Society has funded more than 13,000 research, exploration, and preservation projects around the world. National Geographic Partners distributes a portion of the funds it receives from your purchase to National Geographic Society to support programs including the conservation of animals and their habitats.

National Geographic Partners
1145 17th Street NW
Washington, DC 20036-4688 USA

Get closer to National Geographic explorers and photographers, and connect with our global community. Join us today at nationalgeographic.com/join

For information about special discounts for bulk purchases, please contact National Geographic Books Special Sales: specialsales@natgeo.com

For rights or permissions inquiries, please contact National Geographic Books Subsidiary Rights: bookrights@natgeo.com

Library of Congress Cataloging-in-Publication Data
Names: Thiessen, Mark (Photographer), writer of foreword.
 I National Geographic Society (U.S.)
Title: National geographic spectacle : rare and astonishing
 photographs / foreword by Mark Thiessen.
Description: Washington, D.C. : National Geographic, 2018.
Identifiers: LCCN 2018010224 I ISBN 9781426219689 (hardback)
Subjects: LCSH: Travel photography. I Documentary photography.
 I National Geographic Society (U.S.)--Photograph collections.
 I National geographic. I BISAC: PHOTOGRAPHY / Subjects &
 Themes / Plants & Animals. I PHOTOGRAPHY / Photojournalism.
 I PHOTOGRAPHY / Subjects & Themes / Celebrations & Events.
Classification: LCC TR790 .N3656 2018 I DDC 770--dc23
LC record available at https://lccn.loc.gov_2018010224

Printed in China

18/PPS/1

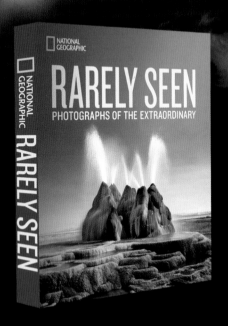
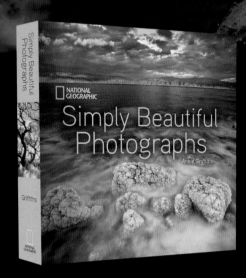
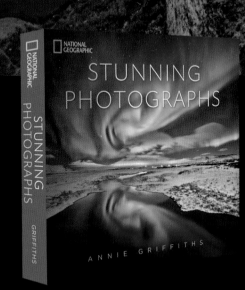